DOVER·THRIFT·EDITIONS

Selected Poems

ALFRED, LORD TENNYSON

DOVER PUBLICATIONS, INC.
New York

DOVER THRIFT EDITIONS
Editor: Stanley Appelbaum

Copyright © 1992 by Dover Publications, Inc.
All rights reserved under Pan American and International Copyright Conventions.

Published in Canada by General Publishing Company, Ltd., 30 Lesmill Road, Don Mills, Toronto, Ontario.
Published in the United Kingdom by Constable and Company, Ltd., 3 The Lanchesters, 162–164 Fulham Palace Road, London W6 9ER.

This Dover edition, first published in 1992, is a new selection of poems, reprinted from *The Poetic and Dramatic Works of Alfred Lord Tennyson: Cambridge Edition*, published by the Houghton Mifflin Company, Boston (The Riverside Press, Cambridge) in 1898. The Note and the alphabetical lists of titles and first names have been prepared specially for the present edition.

Manufactured in the United States of America
Dover Publications, Inc., 31 East 2nd Street, Mineola, N.Y. 11501

Library of Congress Cataloging-in-Publication Data

Tennyson, Alfred Tennyson, Baron, 1809–1892.
   [Poems. Selections]
   Selected poems / Alfred, Lord Tennyson.
      p.   cm.—(Dover thrift editions)
  "Reprinted from The Poetic and dramatic works of Alfred Lord Tennyson: Cambridge edition, published by the Houghton Mifflin Company, Boston . . . in 1898" — T.p. verso.
   Includes indexes.
   ISBN 0-486-27282-6 (pbk.)
   I. Title. II. Series.
PR5553   1992
821'.8—dc20
                                                                     92-29396
                                                                       CIP

Note

ALFRED TENNYSON (1809–1892; a peer from 1884) was the most popular English poet of the Victorian era, combining serious thought with marvelous technical prowess and producing gems even at the very end of his extremely long career. The finest part of his poetic legacy is very much alive, and he is still one of the most frequently quoted English writers. A brief anthology like the present one cannot of course include such lengthy masterworks as "In Memoriam" or *Idylls of the King*, but we have included one famous long narrative poem, "Enoch Arden," as well as a number of important lyrics, monologues, ballads and other typical works. The Dover Thrift Editions normally offer only unabridged pieces, but in the case of Tennyson we are following a long tradition when we isolate individual songs from the long poem "The Princess"; print the quatrains, only, from "The Brook"; and represent the long poem "Maud" merely by the section "Come into the garden, Maud." Tennyson frequently revised earlier poems of his, especially when preparing his successive collected editions. This Dover volume offers the definitive text in each case. The table of contents indicates years of first publication and of revision.

Contents

The subdivisions and sequence are those of the collected editions established by the poet late in life. The dates are those of absolute first publication (whether in periodicals or in volumes), except where otherwise stated.

    page

Juvenilia

    Mariana (1830; revised up to 1860)   1

The Lady of Shalott, and Other Poems

    The Lady of Shalott (1833; revised 1842)   3
    Œnone (1833; revised 1842)   7
    Lady Clara Vere de Vere (written 1833; printed 1842)   14
    The May Queen (1833; "Conclusion" added 1842)   16
    The Lotos-Eaters (1833; revised 1842)   20

English Idyls, and Other Poems

    Ulysses (1842)   25
    Tithonus (1860)   27
    Locksley Hall (1842; slightly revised 1845)   29
    Saint Agnes' Eve (1837; original title "Saint Agnes")   35
    The Beggar Maid (1842)   36
    "Break, break, break" (1842)   36

[Songs from] The Princess; A Medley

"Sweet and low, sweet and low" (1850)	37
"The splendor falls on castle walls" (1850)	37
"Tears, idle tears, I know not what they mean" (1847)	38
"O Swallow, Swallow, flying, flying south" (1847)	38
"Home they brought her warrior dead" (1850)	39
"Now sleeps the crimson petal, now the white" (1847)	39
"Come down, O maid, from yonder mountain height" (1847)	40

Maud, and Other Poems

"Come into the garden, Maud" (Part I, Section xxii, of "Maud: A Monodrama," 1855 with later revisions)	41
The Song of the Brook (the quatrains from "The Brook," 1855)	43
Ode on the Death of the Duke of Wellington (1852)	44
The Charge of the Light Brigade (1854; revised 1855)	52

Enoch Arden, and Other Poems

Enoch Arden (1864)	53
"Flower in the crannied wall" (1869)	76

Ballads, and Other Poems

Rizpah (1880)	76
The Revenge (1878; original title "Sir Richard Grenville")	80

Tiresias, and Other Poems

To Virgil (1882)	84

Demeter, and Other Poems

Merlin and the Gleam (1889)	85
Crossing the Bar (1889)	89

Alphabetical List of Titles   91

Alphabetical List of First Lines   93

Selected Poems

Mariana

'Mariana in the moated grange.'
                          Measure for Measure.

WITH blackest moss the flower-plots
    Were thickly crusted, one and all;
The rusted nails fell from the knots
    That held the pear to the gable-wall.
The broken sheds look'd sad and strange:
    Unlifted was the clinking latch;
    Weeded and worn the ancient thatch
Upon the lonely moated grange.
        She only said, 'My life is dreary,
            He cometh not,' she said;
        She said, 'I am aweary, aweary,
            I would that I were dead!'

Her tears fell with the dews at even;
    Her tears fell ere the dews were dried;
She could not look on the sweet heaven,
    Either at morn or eventide.
After the flitting of the bats,
    When thickest dark did trance the sky,
    She drew her casement-curtain by,
And glanced athwart the glooming flats.
        She only said, 'The night is dreary,
            He cometh not,' she said;
        She said, 'I am aweary, aweary,
            I would that I were dead!'

Upon the middle of the night,
    Waking she heard the night-fowl crow;
The cock sung out an hour ere light;
    From the dark fen the oxen's low
Came to her; without hope of change,
    In sleep she seem'd to walk forlorn,
    Till cold winds woke the gray-eyed morn

About the lonely moated grange.
    She only said, 'The day is dreary,
      He cometh not,' she said;
    She said, 'I am aweary, aweary,
      I would that I were dead !'

About a stone-cast from the wall
  A sluice with blacken'd waters slept,
And o'er it many, round and small,
  The cluster'd marish-mosses crept.
Hard by a poplar shook alway,
  All silver-green with gnarled bark:
For leagues no other tree did mark
The level waste, the rounding gray.
    She only said, 'My life is dreary,
      He cometh not,' she said;
    She said, 'I am aweary, aweary,
      I would that I were dead !'

And ever when the moon was low,
  And the shrill winds were up and away,
In the white curtain, to and fro,
  She saw the gusty shadow sway.
But when the moon was very low,
  And wild winds bound within their cell,
The shadow of the poplar fell
Upon her bed, across her brow.
    She only said, 'The night is dreary,
      He cometh not,' she said;
    She said, 'I am aweary, aweary,
      I would that I were dead !'

All day within the dreamy house,
  The doors upon their hinges creak'd;
The blue fly sung in the pane; the mouse
  Behind the mouldering wainscot shriek'd,
Or from the crevice peer'd about.
  Old faces glimmer'd thro' the doors,
  Old footsteps trod the upper floors,
Old voices called her from without.
    She only said, 'My life is dreary,
      He cometh not,' she said;
    She said, 'I am aweary, aweary,
      I would that I were dead !'

The sparrow's chirrup on the roof,
    The slow clock ticking, and the sound
Which to the wooing wind aloof
    The poplar made, did all confound
Her sense; but most she loathed the hour
    When the thick-moted sunbeam lay
    Athwart the chambers, and the day
Was sloping toward his western bower.
        Then said she, 'I am very dreary,
            He will not come,' she said;
        She wept, 'I am aweary, aweary,
            O God, that I were dead!'

The Lady of Shalott

PART I

On either side the river lie
Long fields of barley and of rye,
That clothe the wold and meet the sky;
And thro' the field the road runs by
        To many-tower'd Camelot;
And up and down the people go,
Gazing where the lilies blow
Round an island there below,
        The island of Shalott.

Willows whiten, aspens quiver,
Little breezes dusk and shiver
Thro' the wave that runs for ever
By the island in the river
        Flowing down to Camelot.
Four gray walls, and four gray towers,
Overlook a space of flowers,
And the silent isle imbowers
        The Lady of Shalott.

By the margin, willow-veil'd,
Slide the heavy barges trail'd
By slow horses; and unhail'd
The shallop flitteth silken-sail'd
        Skimming down to Camelot:

But who hath seen her wave her hand?
Or at the casement seen her stand?
Or is she known in all the land,
      The Lady of Shalott?

Only reapers, reaping early
In among the bearded barley,
Hear a song that echoes cheerly
From the river winding clearly,
      Down to tower'd Camelot;
And by the moon the reaper weary,
Piling sheaves in uplands airy,
Listening, whispers ' 'T is the fairy
      Lady of Shalott.'

PART II

There she weaves by night and day
A magic web with colors gay.
She has heard a whisper say,
A curse is on her if she stay
      To look down to Camelot.
She knows not what the curse may be,
And so she weaveth steadily,
And little other care hath she,
      The Lady of Shalott.

And moving thro' a mirror clear
That hangs before her all the year,
Shadows of the world appear.
There she sees the highway near
      Winding down to Camelot;
There the river eddy whirls,
And there the surly village-churls,
And the red cloaks of market girls,
      Pass onward from Shalott.

Sometimes a troop of damsels glad,
An abbot on an ambling pad,
Sometimes a curly shepherd-lad,
Or long-hair'd page in crimson clad,
      Goes by to tower'd Camelot;
And sometimes thro' the mirror blue
The knights come riding two and two:

She hath no loyal knight and true,
      The Lady of Shalott.

But in her web she still delights
To weave the mirror's magic sights,
For often thro' the silent nights
A funeral, with plumes and lights
      And music, went to Camelot;
Or when the moon was overhead,
Came two young lovers lately wed:
'I am half sick of shadows,' said
      The Lady of Shalott.

PART III

A bow-shot from her bower-eaves,
He rode between the barley-sheaves.
The sun came dazzling thro' the leaves,
And flamed upon the brazen greaves
      Of bold Sir Lancelot.
A red-cross knight for ever kneel'd
To a lady in his shield,
That sparkled on the yellow field,
      Beside remote Shalott.

The gemmy bridle glitter'd free,
Like to some branch of stars we see
Hung in the golden Galaxy.
The bridle bells rang merrily
      As he rode down to Camelot;
And from his blazon'd baldric slung
A mighty silver bugle hung,
And as he rode his armor rung,
      Beside remote Shalott.

All in the blue unclouded weather
Thick-jewell'd shone the saddle-leather,
The helmet and the helmet-feather
Burn'd like one burning flame together,
      As he rode down to Camelot;
As often thro' the purple night,
Below the starry clusters bright,
Some bearded meteor, trailing light,
      Moves over still Shalott.

His broad clear brow in sunlight glow'd;
On burnish'd hooves his war-horse trode;
From underneath his helmet flow'd
His coal-black curls as on he rode,
    As he rode down to Camelot.
From the bank and from the river
He flash'd into the crystal mirror,
'Tirra lirra,' by the river
    Sang Sir Lancelot.

She left the web, she left the loom,
She made three paces thro' the room,
She saw the water-lily bloom,
She saw the helmet and the plume,
    She look'd down to Camelot.
Out flew the web and floated wide;
The mirror crack'd from side to side;
'The curse is come upon me,' cried
    The Lady of Shalott.

PART IV

In the stormy east-wind straining,
The pale yellow woods were waning,
The broad stream in his banks complaining,
Heavily the low sky raining
    Over tower'd Camelot;
Down she came and found a boat
Beneath a willow left afloat,
And round about the prow she wrote
    The Lady of Shalott.

And down the river's dim expanse
Like some bold seër in a trance,
Seeing all his own mischance—
With a glassy countenance
    Did she look to Camelot.
And at the closing of the day
She loosed the chain, and down she lay;
The broad stream bore her far away,
    The Lady of Shalott.

Lying, robed in snowy white
That loosely flew to left and right—
The leaves upon her falling light—

Thro' the noises of the night
        She floated down to Camelot;
And as the boat-head wound along
The willowy hills and fields among,
They heard her singing her last song,
        The Lady of Shalott.

Heard a carol, mournful, holy,
Chanted loudly, chanted lowly,
Till her blood was frozen slowly,
And her eyes were darken'd wholly,
        Turn'd to tower'd Camelot.
For ere she reach'd upon the tide
The first house by the water-side,
Singing in her song she died,
        The Lady of Shalott.

Under tower and balcony,
By garden-wall and gallery,
A gleaming shape she floated by,
Dead-pale between the houses high,
        Silent into Camelot.
Out upon the wharfs they came,
Knight and burgher, lord and dame,
And round the prow they read her name,
        The Lady of Shalott.

Who is this ? and what is here ?
And in the lighted palace near
Died the sound of royal cheer;
And they cross'd themselves for fear,
        All the knights at Camelot:
But Lancelot mused a little space;
He said, 'She has a lovely face;
God in his mercy lend her grace,
        The Lady of Shalott.'

Œnone

THERE lies a vale in Ida, lovelier
Than all the valleys of Ionian hills.
The swimming vapor slopes athwart the glen,
Puts forth an arm, and creeps from pine to pine,
And loiters, slowly drawn. On either hand

The lawns and meadow-ledges midway down
Hang rich in flowers, and far below them roars
The long brook falling thro' the cloven ravine
In cataract after cataract to the sea.
Behind the valley topmost Gargarus
Stands up and takes the morning; but in front
The gorges, opening wide apart, reveal
Troas and Ilion's column'd citadel,
The crown of Troas.

             Hither came at noon
Mournful Œnone, wandering forlorn
Of Paris, once her playmate on the hills.
Her cheek had lost the rose, and round her neck
Floated her hair or seem'd to float in rest.
She, leaning on a fragment twined with vine,
Sang to the stillness, till the mountain-shade
Sloped downward to her seat from the upper cliff.

'O mother Ida, many-fountain'd Ida,
Dear mother Ida, harken ere I die.
For now the noonday quiet holds the hill;
The grasshopper is silent in the grass;
The lizard, with his shadow on the stone,
Rests like a shadow, and the winds are dead.
The purple flower droops, the golden bee
Is lily-cradled; I alone awake.
My eyes are full of tears, my heart of love,
My heart is breaking, and my eyes are dim,
And I am all aweary of my life.

'O mother Ida, many-fountain'd Ida,
Dear mother Ida, harken ere I die.
Hear me, O earth, hear me, O hills, O caves
That house the cold crown'd snake! O mountain brooks,
I am the daughter of a River-God,
Hear me, for I will speak, and build up all
My sorrow with my song, as yonder walls
Rose slowly to a music slowly breathed,
A cloud that gather'd shape; for it may be
That, while I speak of it, a little while
My heart may wander from its deeper woe.

'O mother Ida, many-fountain'd Ida,
Dear mother Ida, harken ere I die.
I waited underneath the dawning hills;
Aloft the mountain lawn was dewy-dark,
And dewy dark aloft the mountain pine.
Beautiful Paris, evil-hearted Paris,
Leading a jet-black goat white-horn'd, white-hooved,
Came up from reedy Simois all alone.

'O mother Ida, harken ere I die.
Far-off the torrent call'd me from the cleft;
Far up the solitary morning smote
The streaks of virgin snow. With down-dropt eyes
I sat alone; white-breasted like a star
Fronting the dawn he moved; a leopard skin
Droop'd from his shoulder, but his sunny hair
Cluster'd about his temples like a God's;
And his cheek brighten'd as the foam-bow brightens
When the wind blows the foam, and all my heart
Went forth to embrace him coming ere he came.

'Dear mother Ida, harken ere I die.
He smiled, and opening out his milk-white palm
Disclosed a fruit of pure Hesperian gold,
That smelt ambrosially, and while I look'd
And listen'd, the full-flowing river of speech
Came down upon my heart:
      ' "My own Œnone,
Beautiful-brow'd Œnone, my own soul,
Behold this fruit, whose gleaming rind ingraven
'For the most fair,' would seem to award it thine,
As lovelier than whatever Oread haunt
The knolls of Ida, loveliest in all grace
Of movement, and the charm of married brows."

'Dear mother Ida, harken ere I die.
He prest the blossom of his lips to mine,
And added, "This was cast upon the board,
When all the full-faced presence of the Gods
Ranged in the halls of Peleus; whereupon
Rose feud, with question unto whom 't were due;
But light-foot Iris brought it yester-eve,
Delivering, that to me, by common voice
Elected umpire, Herè comes to-day,

Pallas and Aphrodite, claiming each
This meed of fairest. Thou, within the cave
Behind yon whispering tuft of oldest pine,
Mayst well behold them unbeheld, unheard
Hear all, and see thy Paris judge of Gods."

'Dear mother Ida, harken ere I die.
It was the deep midnoon; one silvery cloud
Had lost his way between the piny sides
Of this long glen. Then to the bower they came,
Naked they came to that smooth-swarded bower,
And at their feet the crocus brake like fire,
Violet, amaracus, and asphodel,
Lotos and lilies; and a wind arose,
And overhead the wandering ivy and vine,
This way and that, in many a wild festoon
Ran riot, garlanding the gnarled boughs
With bunch and berry and flower thro' and thro'.

'O mother Ida, harken ere I die.
On the tree-tops a crested peacock lit,
And o'er him flow'd a golden cloud, and lean'd
Upon him, slowly dropping fragrant dew.
Then first I heard the voice of her to whom
Coming thro' heaven, like a light that grows
Larger and clearer, with one mind the Gods
Rise up for reverence. She to Paris made
Proffer of royal power, ample rule
Unquestion'd, overflowing revenue
Wherewith to embellish state, "from many a vale
And river-sunder'd champaign clothed with corn,
Or labor'd mine undrainable of ore.
Honor," she said, "and homage, tax and toll,
From many an inland town and haven large,
Mast-throng'd beneath her shadowing citadel
In glassy bays among her tallest towers."

'O mother Ida, harken ere I die.
Still she spake on and still she spake of power,
"Which in all action is the end of all;
Power fitted to the season; wisdom-bred
And throned of wisdom—from all neighbor crowns
Alliance and allegiance, till thy hand
Fail from the sceptre-staff. Such boon from me,

From me, heaven's queen, Paris, to thee king-born,
A shepherd all thy life but yet king-born,
Should come most welcome, seeing men, in power
Only, are likest Gods, who have attain'd
Rest in a happy place and quiet seats
Above the thunder, with undying bliss
In knowledge of their own supremacy."

   'Dear mother Ida, harken ere I die.
She ceased, and Paris held the costly fruit
Out at arm's-length, so much the thought of power
Flatter'd his spirit; but Pallas where she stood
Somewhat apart, her clear and bared limbs
O'erthwarted with the brazen-headed spear
Upon her pearly shoulder leaning cold,
The while, above, her full and earnest eye
Over her snow-cold breast and angry cheek
Kept watch, waiting decision, made reply:

  ' "Self-reverence, self-knowledge, self-control,
These three alone lead life to sovereign power.
Yet not for power (power of herself
Would come uncall'd for) but to live by law,
Acting the law we live by without fear;
And, because right is right, to follow right
Were wisdom in the scorn of consequence."

  'Dear mother Ida, harken ere I die.
Again she said: "I woo thee not with gifts.
Sequel of guerdon could not alter me
To fairer. Judge thou me by what I am,
So shalt thou find me fairest.
                            Yet, indeed,
If gazing on divinity disrobed
Thy mortal eyes are frail to judge of fair,
Unbias'd by self-profit, O, rest thee sure
That I shall love thee well and cleave to thee,
So that my vigor, wedded to thy blood,
Shall strike within thy pulses, like a God's,
To push thee forward thro' a life of shocks,
Dangers, and deeds, until endurance grow
Sinew'd with action, and the full-grown will,
Circled thro' all experiences, pure law,
Commeasure perfect freedom."

'Here she ceas'd,
And Paris ponder'd, and I cried, "O Paris,
Give it to Pallas!" but he heard me not,
Or hearing would not hear me, woe is me!

'O mother Ida, many-fountain'd Ida,
Dear mother Ida, harken ere I die.
Idalian Aphrodite beautiful,
Fresh as the foam, new-bathed in Paphian wells,
With rosy slender fingers backward drew
From her warm brows and bosom her deep hair
Ambrosial, golden round her lucid throat
And shoulder; from the violets her light foot
Shone rosy-white, and o'er her rounded form
Between the shadows of the vine-bunches
Floated the glowing sunlights, as she moved.

'Dear mother Ida, harken ere I die.
She with a subtle smile in her mild eyes,
The herald of her triumph, drawing nigh
Half-whisper'd in his ear, "I promise thee
The fairest and most loving wife in Greece."
She spoke and laugh'd; I shut my sight for fear;
But when I look'd, Paris had raised his arm,
And I beheld great Herè's angry eyes,
As she withdrew into the golden cloud,
And I was left alone within the bower;
And from that time to this I am alone,
And I shall be alone until I die.

'Yet, mother Ida, harken ere I die.
Fairest—why fairest wife? am I not fair?
My love hath told me so a thousand times.
Methinks I must be fair, for yesterday,
When I past by, a wild and wanton pard,
Eyed like the evening star, with playful tail
Crouch'd fawning in the weed. Most loving is she?
Ah me, my mountain shepherd, that my arms
Were wound about thee, and my hot lips prest
Close, close to thine in that quick-falling dew
Of fruitful kisses, thick as autumn rains
Flash in the pools of whirling Simois!

'O mother, hear me yet before I die.
They came, they cut away my tallest pines,

My tall dark pines, that plumed the craggy ledge
High over the blue gorge, and all between
The snowy peak and snow-white cataract
Foster'd the callow eaglet—from beneath
Whose thick mysterious boughs in the dark morn
The panther's roar came muffled, while I sat
Low in the valley. Never, never more
Shall lone Œnone see the morning mist
Sweep thro' them; never see them overlaid
With narrow moonlit slips of silver cloud,
Between the loud stream and the trembling stars.

   'O mother, hear me yet before I die.
I wish that somewhere in the ruin'd folds,
Among the fragments tumbled from the glens,
Or the dry thickets, I could meet with her
The Abominable, that uninvited came
Into the fair Peleïan banquet-hall,
And cast the golden fruit upon the board,
And bred this change; that I might speak my mind,
And tell her to her face how much I hate
Her presence, hated both of Gods and men.

   'O mother, hear me yet before I die.
Hath he not sworn his love a thousand times,
In this green valley, under this green hill,
Even on this hand, and sitting on this stone?
Seal'd it with kisses? water'd it with tears?
O happy tears, and how unlike to these!
O happy heaven, how canst thou see my face?
O happy earth, how canst thou bear my weight?
O death, death, death, thou ever-floating cloud,
There are enough unhappy on this earth,
Pass by the happy souls, that love to live;
I pray thee, pass before my light of life,
And shadow all my soul, that I may die.
Thou weighest heavy on the heart within,
Weigh heavy on my eyelids; let me die.

   'O mother, hear me yet before I die.
I will not die alone, for fiery thoughts
Do shape themselves within me, more and more,
Whereof I catch the issue, as I hear
Dead sounds at night come from the inmost hills,

Like footsteps upon wool. I dimly see
My far-off doubtful purpose, as a mother
Conjectures of the features of her child
Ere it is born. Her child!—a shudder comes
Across me: never child be born of me,
Unblest, to vex me with his father's eyes!

'O mother, hear me yet before I die.
Hear me, O earth. I will not die alone,
Lest their shrill happy laughter come to me
Walking the cold and starless road of death
Uncomforted, leaving my ancient love
With the Greek woman. I will rise and go
Down into Troy, and ere the stars come forth
Talk with the wild Cassandra, for she says
A fire dances before her, and a sound
Rings ever in her ears of armèd men.
What this may be I know not, but I know
That, wheresoe'er I am by night and day,
All earth and air seem only burning fire.'

Lady Clara Vere de Vere

LADY Clara Vere de Vere,
   Of me you shall not win renown:
You thought to break a country heart
   For pastime, ere you went to town.
At me you smiled, but unbeguiled
   I saw the snare, and I retired;
The daughter of a hundred earls,
   You are not one to be desired.

Lady Clara Vere de Vere,
   I know you proud to bear your name,
Your pride is yet no mate for mine,
   Too proud to care from whence I came.
Nor would I break for your sweet sake
   A heart that dotes on truer charms.
A simple maiden in her flower
   Is worth a hundred coats-of-arms.

Lady Clara Vere de Vere,
   Some meeker pupil you must find,

For, were you queen of all that is,
    I could not stoop to such a mind.
You sought to prove how I could love,
    And my disdain is my reply.
The lion on your old stone gates
    Is not more cold to you than I.

Lady Clara Vere de Vere,
    You put strange memories in my head.
Not thrice your branching limes have blown
    Since I beheld young Laurence dead.
O, your sweet eyes, your low replies!
    A great enchantress you may be;
But there was that across his throat
    Which you had hardly cared to see.

Lady Clara Vere de Vere,
    When thus he met his mother's view,
She had the passions of her kind,
    She spake some certain truths of you.
Indeed I heard one bitter word
    That scarce is fit for you to hear;
Her manners had not that repose
    Which stamps the caste of Vere de Vere.

Lady Clara Vere de Vere,
    There stands a spectre in your hall;
The guilt of blood is at your door;
    You changed a wholesome heart to gall.
You held your course without remorse,
    To make him trust his modest worth,
And, last, you fix'd a vacant stare,
    And slew him with your noble birth.

Trust me, Clara Vere de Vere,
    From yon blue heavens above us bent
The gardener Adam and his wife
    Smile at the claims of long descent.
Howe'er it be, it seems to me,
    'T is only noble to be good.
Kind hearts are more than coronets,
    And simple faith than Norman blood.

I know you, Clara Vere de Vere,
    You pine among your halls and towers;

The languid light of your proud eyes
    Is wearied of the rolling hours.
In glowing health, with boundless wealth,
    But sickening of a vague disease,
You know so ill to deal with time,
    You needs must play such pranks as these.

Clara, Clara Vere de Vere,
    If time be heavy on your hands,
Are there no beggars at your gate,
    Nor any poor about your lands?
O, teach the orphan-boy to read,
    Or teach the orphan-girl to sew;
Pray Heaven for a human heart,
    And let the foolish yeoman go.

The May Queen

You must wake and call me early, call me early, mother dear;
To-morrow 'ill be the happiest time of all the glad New-year;
Of all the glad New-year, mother, the maddest merriest day,
For I'm to be Queen o' the May, mother, I'm to be Queen o' the May.

There's many a black, black eye, they say, but none so bright as mine;
There's Margaret and Mary, there's Kate and Caroline;
But none so fair as little Alice in all the land they say,
So I'm to be Queen o' the May, mother, I'm to be Queen o' the May.

I sleep so sound all night, mother, that I shall never wake,
If you do not call me loud when the day begins to break;
But I must gather knots of flowers, and buds and garlands gay,
For I'm to be Queen o' the May, mother, I'm to be Queen o' the May.

As I came up the valley whom think ye should I see
But Robin leaning on the bridge beneath the hazel-tree?
He thought of that sharp look, mother, I gave him yesterday,
But I'm to be Queen o' the May, mother, I'm to be Queen o' the May.

He thought I was a ghost, mother, for I was all in white,
And I ran by him without speaking, like a flash of light.
They call me cruel-hearted, but I care not what they say,
For I'm to be Queen o' the May, mother, I'm to be Queen o' the May.

They say he's dying all for love, but that can never be;
They say his heart is breaking, mother—what is that to me?

There's many a bolder lad 'ill woo me any summer day,
And I'm to be Queen o' the May, mother, I'm to be Queen o' the May.

Little Effie shall go with me to-morrow to the green,
And you'll be there, too, mother, to see me made the Queen;
For the shepherd lads on every side 'ill come from far away,
And I'm to be Queen o' the May, mother, I'm to be Queen o' the May.

The honeysuckle round the porch has woven its wavy bowers,
And by the meadow-trenches blow the faint sweet cuckoo-flowers;
And the wild marsh-marigold shines like fire in swamps and hollows gray,
And I'm to be Queen o' the May, mother, I'm to be Queen o' the May.

The night-winds come and go, mother, upon the meadow-grass,
And the happy stars above them seem to brighten as they pass;
There will not be a drop of rain the whole of the livelong day,
And I'm to be Queen o' the May, mother, I'm to be Queen o' the May.

All the valley, mother, 'ill be fresh and green and still,
And the cowslip and the crowfoot are over all the hill,
And the rivulet in the flowery dale 'ill merrily glance and play,
For I'm to be Queen o' the May, mother, I'm to be Queen o' the May.

So you must wake and call me early, call me early, mother dear,
To-morrow 'ill be the happiest time of all the glad New-year;
To-morrow 'ill be of all the year the maddest merriest day,
For I'm to be Queen o' the May, mother, I'm to be Queen o' the May.

NEW-YEAR'S EVE

IF you're waking call me early, call me early, mother dear,
For I would see the sun rise upon the glad New-year.
It is the last New-year that I shall ever see,
Then you may lay me low i' the mould and think no more of me.

To-night I saw the sun set; he set and left behind
The good old year, the dear old time, and all my peace of mind;
And the New-year's coming up, mother, but I shall never see
The blossom on the blackthorn, the leaf upon the tree.

Last May we made a crown of flowers; we had a merry day;
Beneath the hawthorn on the green they made me Queen of May;
And we danced about the may-pole and in the hazel copse,
Till Charles's Wain came out above the tall white chimney-tops.

There's not a flower on all the hills; the frost is on the pane.
I only wish to live till the snowdrops come again;

I wish the snow would melt and the sun come out on high;
I long to see a flower so before the day I die.

The building rook 'll caw from the windy tall elm-tree,
And the tufted plover pipe along the fallow lea,
And the swallow 'ill come back again with summer o'er the wave,
But I shall lie alone, mother, within the mouldering grave.

Upon the chancel-casement, and upon that grave of mine,
In the early early morning the summer sun 'ill shine,
Before the red cock crows from the farm upon the hill,
When you are warm-asleep, mother, and all the world is still.

When the flowers come again, mother, beneath the waning light
You'll never see me more in the long gray fields at night;
When from the dry dark wold the summer airs blow cool
On the oat-grass and the sword-grass, and the bulrush in the pool.

You'll bury me, my mother, just beneath the hawthorn shade,
And you'll come sometimes and see me where I am lowly laid.
I shall not forget you, mother, I shall hear you when you pass,
With your feet above my head in the long and pleasant grass.

I have been wild and wayward, but you'll forgive me now;
You'll kiss me, my own mother, and forgive me ere I go;
Nay, nay, you must not weep, nor let your grief be wild;
You should not fret for me, mother, you have another child.

If I can I'll come again, mother, from out my resting-place;
Tho' you'll not see me, mother, I shall look upon your face;
Tho' I cannot speak a word, I shall harken what you say,
And be often, often with you when you think I'm far away.

Good-night, good-night, when I have said good-night for evermore,
And you see me carried out from the threshold of the door,
Don't let Effie come to see me till my grave be growing green.
She'll be a better child to you than ever I have been.

She'll find my garden-tools upon the granary floor.
Let her take 'em, they are hers; I shall never garden more;
But tell her, when I'm gone, to train the rosebush that I set
About the parlor-window and the box of mignonette.

Good-night, sweet mother; call me before the day is born.
All night I lie awake, but I fall asleep at morn;

But I would see the sun rise upon the glad New-year,
So, if you're waking, call me, call me early, mother dear.

CONCLUSION

I THOUGHT to pass away before, and yet alive I am;
And in the fields all round I hear the bleating of the lamb.
How sadly, I remember, rose the morning of the year !
To die before the snowdrop came, and now the violet's here.

O, sweet is the new violet, that comes beneath the skies,
And sweeter is the young lamb's voice to me that cannot rise,
And sweet is all the land about, and all the flowers that blow,
And sweeter far is death than life to me that long to go.

It seem'd so hard at first, mother, to leave the blessed sun,
And now it seems as hard to stay, and yet His will be done !
But still I think it can't be long before I find release;
And that good man, the clergyman, has told me words of peace.

O, blessings on his kindly voice and on his silver hair !
And blessings on his whole life long, until he meet me there !
O, blessings on his kindly heart and on his silver head !
A thousand times I blest him, as he knelt beside my bed.

He taught me all the mercy, for he show'd me all the sin.
Now, tho' my lamp was lighted late, there's One will let me in;
Nor would I now be well, mother, again, if that could be,
For my desire is but to pass to Him that died for me.

I did not hear the dog howl, mother, or the death-watch beat,
There came a sweeter token when the night and morning meet;
But sit beside my bed, mother, and put your hand in mine,
And Effie on the other side, and I will tell the sign.

All in the wild March-morning I heard the angels call;
It was when the moon was setting, and the dark was over all;
The trees began to whisper, and the wind began to roll,
And in the wild March-morning I heard them call my soul.

For lying broad awake I thought of you and Effie dear;
I saw you sitting in the house, and I no longer here;
With all my strength I pray'd for both, and so I felt resign'd,
And up the valley came a swell of music on the wind.

I thought that it was fancy, and I listen'd in my bed,
And then did something speak to me—I know not what was said;

For great delight and shuddering took hold of all my mind,
And up the valley came again the music on the wind.

But you were sleeping; and I said, 'It's not for them, it's mine.'
And if it come three times, I thought, I take it for a sign.
And once again it came, and close beside the window-bars,
Then seem'd to go right up to heaven and die among the stars.

So now I think my time is near. I trust it is. I know
The blessed music went that way my soul will have to go.
And for myself, indeed, I care not if I go to-day;
But, Effie, you must comfort *her* when I am past away.

And say to Robin a kind word, and tell him not to fret;
There's many a worthier than I, would make him happy yet.
If I had lived—I cannot tell—I might have been his wife;
But all these things have ceased to be, with my desire of life.

O, look! the sun begins to rise, the heavens are in a glow;
He shines upon a hundred fields, and all of them I know.
And there I move no longer now, and there his light may shine—
Wild flowers in the valley for other hands than mine.

O, sweet and strange it seems to me, that ere this day is done
The voice, that now is speaking, may be beyond the sun—
For ever and for ever with those just souls and true—
And what is life, that we should moan? why make we such ado?

For ever and for ever, all in a blessed home—
And there to wait a little while till you and Effie come—
To lie within the light of God, as I lie upon your breast—
And the wicked cease from troubling, and the weary are at rest.

The Lotos-Eaters

'COURAGE!' he said, and pointed toward the land,
'This mounting wave will roll us shoreward soon.'
In the afternoon they came unto a land
In which it seemed always afternoon.
All round the coast the languid air did swoon,
Breathing like one that hath a weary dream.
Full-faced above the valley stood the moon;
And, like a downward smoke, the slender stream
Along the cliff to fall and pause and fall did seem.

A land of streams! some, like a downward smoke,
Slow-dropping veils of thinnest lawn, did go;
And some thro' wavering lights and shadows broke,
Rolling a slumbrous sheet of foam below.
They saw the gleaming river seaward flow
From the inner land; far off, three mountain-tops,
Three silent pinnacles of aged snow,
Stood sunset-flush'd; and, dew'd with showery drops,
Up-clomb the shadowy pine above the woven copse.

The charmed sunset linger'd low adown
In the red West; thro' mountain clefts the dale
Was seen far inland, and the yellow down
Border'd with palm, and many a winding vale
And meadow, set with slender galingale;
A land where all things always seem'd the same!
And round about the keel with faces pale,
Dark faces pale against that rosy flame,
The mild-eyed melancholy Lotos-eaters came.

Branches they bore of that enchanted stem,
Laden with flower and fruit, whereof they gave
To each, but whoso did receive of them
And taste, to him the gushing of the wave
Far far away did seem to mourn and rave
On alien shores; and if his fellow spake,
His voice was thin, as voices from the grave;
And deep-asleep he seem'd, yet all awake,
And music in his ears his beating heart did make.

They sat them down upon the yellow sand,
Between the sun and moon upon the shore;
And sweet it was to dream of Fatherland,
Of child, and wife, and slave; but evermore
Most weary seem'd the sea, weary the oar,
Weary the wandering fields of barren foam.
Then some one said, 'We will return no more;'
And all at once they sang, 'Our island home
Is far beyond the wave; we will no longer roam.'

CHORIC SONG

I

There is sweet music here that softer falls
Than petals from blown roses on the grass,

Or night-dews on still waters between walls
Of shadowy granite, in a gleaming pass;
Music that gentlier on the spirit lies,
Than tired eyelids upon tired eyes;
Music that brings sweet sleep down from the blissful skies.
Here are cool mosses deep,
And thro' the moss the ivies creep,
And in the stream the long-leaved flowers weep,
And from the craggy ledge the poppy hangs in sleep.

II

Why are we weigh'd upon with heaviness,
And utterly consumed with sharp distress,
While all things else have rest from weariness?
All things have rest: why should we toil alone,
We only toil, who are the first of things,
And make perpetual moan,
Still from one sorrow to another thrown;
Nor ever fold our wings,
And cease from wanderings,
Nor steep our brows in slumber's holy balm;
Nor harken what the inner spirit sings,
'There is no joy but calm!'—
Why should we only toil, the roof and crown of things?

III

Lo! in the middle of the wood,
The folded leaf is woo'd from out the bud
With winds upon the branch, and there
Grows green and broad, and takes no care,
Sun-steep'd at noon, and in the moon
Nightly dew-fed; and turning yellow
Falls, and floats adown the air.
Lo! sweeten'd with the summer light,
The full-juiced apple, waxing over-mellow,
Drops in a silent autumn night.
All its allotted length of days
The flower ripens in its place,
Ripens and fades, and falls, and hath no toil,
Fast-rooted in the fruitful soil.

IV

Hateful is the dark-blue sky,
Vaulted o'er the dark-blue sea.
Death is the end of life; ah, why
Should life all labor be?
Let us alone. Time driveth onward fast,
And in a little while our lips are dumb.
Let us alone. What is it that will last?
All things are taken from us, and become
Portions and parcels of the dreadful past.
Let us alone. What pleasure can we have
To war with evil? Is there any peace
In ever climbing up the climbing wave?
All things have rest, and ripen toward the grave
In silence—ripen, fall, and cease:
Give us long rest or death, dark death, or dreamful ease.

V

How sweet it were, hearing the downward stream,
With half-shut eyes ever to seem
Falling asleep in a half-dream!
To dream and dream, like yonder amber light,
Which will not leave the myrrh-bush on the height;
To hear each other's whisper'd speech;
Eating the Lotos day by day,
To watch the crisping ripples on the beach,
And tender curving lines of creamy spray;
To lend our hearts and spirits wholly
To the influence of mild-minded melancholy;
To muse and brood and live again in memory,
With those old faces of our infancy
Heap'd over with a mound of grass,
Two handfuls of white dust, shut in an urn of brass!

VI

Dear is the memory of our wedded lives,
And dear the last embraces of our wives
And their warm tears; but all hath suffer'd change;
For surely now our household hearths are cold,
Our sons inherit us, our looks are strange,

And we should come like ghosts to trouble joy.
Or else the island princes over-bold
Have eat our substance, and the minstrel sings
Before them of the ten years' war in Troy,
And our great deeds, as half-forgotten things.
Is there confusion in the little isle?
Let what is broken so remain.
The Gods are hard to reconcile;
'T is hard to settle order once again.
There *is* confusion worse than death,
Trouble on trouble, pain on pain,
Long labor unto aged breath,
Sore task to hearts worn out by many wars
And eyes grown dim with gazing on the pilot-stars.

VII

But, propt on beds of amaranth and moly,
How sweet—while warm airs lull us, blowing lowly—
With half-dropt eyelid still,
Beneath a heaven dark and holy,
To watch the long bright river drawing slowly
His waters from the purple hill—
To hear the dewy echoes calling
From cave to cave thro' the thick-twined vine—
To watch the emerald-color'd water falling
Thro' many a woven acanthus-wreath divine!
Only to hear and see the far-off sparkling brine,
Only to hear were sweet, stretch'd out beneath the pine.

VIII

The Lotos blooms below the barren peak,
The Lotos blows by every winding creek;
All day the wind breathes low with mellower tone;
Thro' every hollow cave and alley lone
Round and round the spicy downs the yellow Lotos-dust is blown.
We have had enough of action, and of motion we,
Roll'd to starboard, roll'd to larboard, when the surge was seething free,
Where the wallowing monster spouted his foam-fountains in the sea.
Let us swear an oath, and keep it with an equal mind,
In the hollow Lotos-land to live and lie reclined
On the hills like Gods together, careless of mankind.

For they lie beside their nectar, and the bolts are hurl'd
Far below them in the valleys, and the clouds are lightly curl'd
Round their golden houses, girdled with the gleaming world;
Where they smile in secret, looking over wasted lands,
Blight and famine, plague and earthquake, roaring deeps and fiery sands,
Clanging fights, and flaming towns, and sinking ships, and praying hands.
But they smile, they find a music centred in a doleful song
Steaming up, a lamentation and an ancient tale of wrong,
Like a tale of little meaning tho' the words are strong;
Chanted from an ill-used race of men that cleave the soil,
Sow the seed, and reap the harvest with enduring toil,
Storing yearly little dues of wheat, and wine and oil;
Till they perish and they suffer—some, 't is whisper'd—down in hell
Suffer endless anguish, others in Elysian valleys dwell,
Resting weary limbs at last on beds of asphodel.
Surely, surely, slumber is more sweet than toil, the shore
Than labor in the deep mid-ocean, wind and wave and oar;
O, rest ye, brother mariners, we will not wander more.

Ulysses

It little profits that an idle king,
By this still hearth, among these barren crags,
Match'd with an aged wife, I mete and dole
Unequal laws unto a savage race,
That hoard, and sleep, and feed, and know not me.
I cannot rest from travel; I will drink
Life to the lees. All times I have enjoy'd
Greatly, have suffer'd greatly, both with those
That loved me, and alone; on shore, and when
Thro' scudding drifts the rainy Hyades
Vext the dim sea. I am become a name;
For always roaming with a hungry heart
Much have I seen and known,—cities of men
And manners, climates, councils, governments,
Myself not least, but honor'd of them all,—
And drunk delight of battle with my peers,
Far on the ringing plains of windy Troy.
I am a part of all that I have met;

Yet all experience is an arch wherethro'
Gleams that untravell'd world whose margin fades
For ever and for ever when I move.
How dull it is to pause, to make an end,
To rust unburnish'd, not to shine in use !
As tho' to breathe were life ! Life piled on life
Were all too little, and of one to me
Little remains; but every hour is saved
From that eternal silence, something more,
A bringer of new things; and vile it were
For some three suns to store and hoard myself,
And this gray spirit yearning in desire
To follow knowledge like a sinking star,
Beyond the utmost bound of human thought.

    This is my son, mine own Telemachus,
To whom I leave the sceptre and the isle,—
Well-loved of me, discerning to fulfil
This labor, by slow prudence to make mild
A rugged people, and thro' soft degrees
Subdue them to the useful and the good.
Most blameless is he, centred in the sphere
Of common duties, decent not to fail
In offices of tenderness, and pay
Meet adoration to my household gods,
When I am gone. He works his work, I mine.

    There lies the port; the vessel puffs her sail;
There gloom the dark, broad seas. My mariners,
Souls that have toil'd, and wrought, and thought with me,—
That ever with a frolic welcome took
The thunder and the sunshine, and opposed
Free hearts, free foreheads,—you and I are old;
Old age hath yet his honor and his toil.
Death closes all; but something ere the end,
Some work of noble note, may yet be done,
Not unbecoming men that strove with Gods.
The lights begin to twinkle from the rocks;
The long day wanes; the slow moon climbs; the deep
Moans round with many voices. Come, my friends.
'T is not too late to seek a newer world.
Push off, and sitting well in order smite
The sounding furrows; for my purpose holds
To sail beyond the sunset, and the baths
Of all the western stars, until I die.

It may be that the gulfs will wash us down;
It may be we shall touch the Happy Isles,
And see the great Achilles, whom we knew.
Tho' much is taken, much abides; and tho'
We are not now that strength which in old days
Moved earth and heaven, that which we are, we are,—
One equal temper of heroic hearts,
Made weak by time and fate, but strong in will
To strive, to seek, to find, and not to yield.

Tithonus

THE woods decay, the woods decay and fall,
The vapors weep their burthen to the ground.
Man comes and tills the field and lies beneath,
And after many a summer dies the swan.
Me only cruel immortality
Consumes; I wither slowly in thine arms,
Here at the quiet limit of the world,
A white-hair'd shadow roaming like a dream
The ever-silent spaces of the East,
Far-folded mists, and gleaming halls of morn.
  Alas! for this gray shadow, once a man—
So glorious in his beauty and thy choice,
Who madest him thy chosen, that he seem'd
To his great heart none other than a God!
I ask'd thee, 'Give me immortality.'
Then didst thou grant mine asking with a smile,
Like wealthy men who care not how they give.
But thy strong Hours indignant work'd their wills,
And beat me down and marr'd and wasted me,
And tho' they could not end me, left me maim'd
To dwell in presence of immortal youth,
Immortal age beside immortal youth,
And all I was in ashes. Can thy love,
Thy beauty, make amends, tho' even now,
Close over us, the silver star, thy guide,
Shines in those tremulous eyes that fill with tears
To hear me? Let me go; take back thy gift.
Why should a man desire in any way
To vary from the kindly race of men,
Or pass beyond the goal of ordinance

Where all should pause, as is most meet for all ?
    A soft air fans the cloud apart; there comes
A glimpse of that dark world where I was born.
Once more the old mysterious glimmer steals
From thy pure brows, and from thy shoulders pure,
And bosom beating with a heart renew'd.
Thy cheek begins to redden thro' the gloom,
Thy sweet eyes brighten slowly close to mine,
Ere yet they blind the stars, and the wild team
Which love thee, yearning for thy yoke, arise,
And shake the darkness from their loosen'd manes,
And beat the twilight into flakes of fire.

    Lo ! ever thus thou growest beautiful
In silence, then before thine answer given
Departest, and thy tears are on my cheek.

    Why wilt thou ever scare me with thy tears,
And make me tremble lest a saying learnt,
In days far-off, on that dark earth, be true ?
'The Gods themselves cannot recall their gifts.'

    Ay me ! ay me ! with what another heart
In days far-off, and with what other eyes
I used to watch—if I be he that watch'd—
The lucid outline forming round thee; saw
The dim curls kindle into sunny rings;
Changed with thy mystic change, and felt my blood
Glow with the glow that slowly crimson'd all
Thy presence and thy portals, while I lay,
Mouth, forehead, eyelids, growing dewy-warm
With kisses balmier than half-opening buds
Of April, and could hear the lips that kiss'd
Whispering I knew not what of wild and sweet,
Like that strange song I heard Apollo sing,
While Ilion like a mist rose into towers.

    Yet hold me not for ever in thine East;
How can my nature longer mix with thine ?
Coldly thy rosy shadows bathe me, cold
Are all thy lights, and cold my wrinkled feet
Upon thy glimmering thresholds, when the steam
Floats up from those dim fields about the homes
Of happy men that have the power to die,
And grassy barrows of the happier dead.
Release me, and restore me to the ground.
Thou seest all things, thou wilt see my grave;

Thou wilt renew thy beauty morn by morn,
I earth in earth forget these empty courts,
And thee returning on thy silver wheels.

Locksley Hall

COMRADES, leave me here a little, while as yet 't is early morn;
Leave me here, and when you want me, sound upon the bugle-horn.

'T is the place, and all around it, as of old, the curlews call,
Dreary gleams about the moorland flying over Locksley Hall;

Locksley Hall, that in the distance overlooks the sandy tracts,
And the hollow ocean-ridges roaring into cataracts.

Many a night from yonder ivied casement, ere I went to rest,
Did I look on great Orion sloping slowly to the west.

Many a night I saw the Pleiads, rising thro' the mellow shade,
Glitter like a swarm of fireflies tangled in a silver braid.

Here about the beach I wander'd, nourishing a youth sublime
With the fairy tales of science, and the long result of time;

When the centuries behind me like a fruitful land reposed;
When I clung to all the present for the promise that it closed;

When I dipt into the future far as human eye could see,
Saw the vision of the world and all the wonder that would be.—

In the spring a fuller crimson comes upon the robin's breast;
In the spring the wanton lapwing gets himself another crest;

In the spring a livelier iris changes on the burnish'd dove;
In the spring a young man's fancy lightly turns to thoughts of love.

Then her cheek was pale and thinner than should be for one so young,
And her eyes on all my motions with a mute observance hung.

And I said, 'My cousin Amy, speak, and speak the truth to me,
Trust me, cousin, all the current of my being sets to thee.'

On her pallid cheek and forehead came a color and a light,
As I have seen the rosy red flushing in the northern night.

And she turn'd—her bosom shaken with a sudden storm of sighs—
All the spirit deeply dawning in the dark of hazel eyes—

Saying, 'I have hid my feelings, fearing they should do me wrong;'
Saying, 'Dost thou love me, cousin?' weeping, 'I have loved thee long.'

Love took up the glass of Time, and turn'd it in his glowing hands;
Every moment, lightly shaken, ran itself in golden sands.

Love took up the harp of Life, and smote on all the chords with might;
Smote the chord of Self, that, trembling, past in music out of sight.

Many a morning on the moorland did we hear the copses ring,
And her whisper throng'd my pulses with the fulness of the spring.

Many an evening by the waters did we watch the stately ships,
And our spirits rush'd together at the touching of the lips.

O my cousin, shallow-hearted! O my Amy, mine no more!
O the dreary, dreary moorland! O the barren, barren shore!

Falser than all fancy fathoms, falser than all songs have sung,
Puppet to a father's threat, and servile to a shrewish tongue!

Is it well to wish thee happy?—having known me—to decline
On a range of lower feelings and a narrower heart than mine!

Yet it shall be; thou shalt lower to his level day by day,
What is fine within thee growing coarse to sympathize with clay.

As the husband is, the wife is; thou art mated with a clown,
And the grossness of his nature will have weight to drag thee down.

He will hold thee, when his passion shall have spent its novel force,
Something better than his dog, a little dearer than his horse.

What is this? his eyes are heavy; think not they are glazed with wine.
Go to him, it is thy duty; kiss him, take his hand in thine.

It may be my lord is weary, that his brain is overwrought;
Soothe him with thy finer fancies, touch him with thy lighter thought.

He will answer to the purpose, easy things to understand—
Better thou wert dead before me, tho' I slew thee with my hand!

Better thou and I were lying, hidden from the heart's disgrace,
Roll'd in one another's arms, and silent in a last embrace.

Cursed be the social wants that sin against the strength of youth!
Cursed be the social lies that warp us from the living truth!

Cursed be the sickly forms that err from honest Nature's rule!
Cursed be the gold that gilds the straiten'd forehead of the fool!

Well—'t is well that I should bluster!—Hadst thou less unworthy proved—
Would to God—for I had loved thee more than ever wife was loved.

Am I mad, that I should cherish that which bears but bitter fruit?
I will pluck it from my bosom, tho' my heart be at the root.

Never, tho' my mortal summers to such length of years should come
As the many-winter'd crow that leads the clanging rookery home.

Where is comfort? in division of the records of the mind?
Can I part her from herself, and love her, as I knew her, kind?

I remember one that perish'd; sweetly did she speak and move;
Such a one do I remember, whom to look at was to love.

Can I think of her as dead, and love her for the love she bore?
No—she never loved me truly; love is love for evermore.

Comfort? comfort scorn'd of devils! this is truth the poet sings,
That a sorrow's crown of sorrow is remembering happier things.

Drug thy memories, lest thou learn it, lest thy heart be put to proof,
In the dead unhappy night, and when the rain is on the roof.

Like a dog, he hunts in dreams, and thou art staring at the wall,
Where the dying night-lamp flickers, and the shadows rise and fall.

Then a hand shall pass before thee, pointing to his drunken sleep,
To thy widow'd marriage-pillows, to the tears that thou wilt weep.

Thou shalt hear the 'Never, never,' whisper'd by the phantom years,
And a song from out the distance in the ringing of thine ears;

And an eye shall vex thee, looking ancient kindness on thy pain.
Turn thee, turn thee on thy pillow; get thee to thy rest again.

Nay, but Nature brings thee solace; for a tender voice will cry.
'T is a purer life than thine, a lip to drain thy trouble dry.

Baby lips will laugh me down; my latest rival brings thee rest.
Baby fingers, waxen touches, press me from the mother's breast.

O, the child too clothes the father with a dearness not his due.
Half is thine and half is his; it will be worthy of the two.

O, I see thee old and formal, fitted to thy petty part,
With a little hoard of maxims preaching down a daughter's heart.

'They were dangerous guides the feelings—she herself was not exempt—
Truly, she herself had suffer'd'—Perish in thy self-contempt!

Overlive it—lower yet—be happy! wherefore should I care?
I myself must mix with action, lest I wither by despair.

What is that which I should turn to, lighting upon days like these?
Every door is barr'd with gold, and opens but to golden keys.

Every gate is throng'd with suitors, all the markets overflow.
I have but an angry fancy; what is that which I should do?

I had been content to perish, falling on the foeman's ground,
When the ranks are roll'd in vapor, and the winds are laid with sound.

But the jingling of the guinea helps the hurt that Honor feels,
And the nations do but murmur, snarling at each other's heels.

Can I but relive in sadness? I will turn that earlier page.
Hide me from my deep emotion, O thou wondrous Mother-Age!

Make me feel the wild pulsation that I felt before the strife,
When I heard my days before me, and the tumult of my life;

Yearning for the large excitement that the coming years would yield,
Eager-hearted as a boy when first he leaves his father's field,

And at night along the dusky highway near and nearer drawn,
Sees in heaven the light of London flaring like a dreary dawn;

And his spirit leaps within him to be gone before him then,
Underneath the light he looks at, in among the throngs of men;

Men, my brothers, men the workers, ever reaping something new;
That which they have done but earnest of the things that they shall do.

For I dipt into the future, far as human eye could see,
Saw the Vision of the world, and all the wonder that would be;

Saw the heavens fill with commerce, argosies of magic sails,
Pilots of the purple twilight, dropping down with costly bales;

Heard the heavens fill with shouting, and there rain'd a ghastly dew
From the nations' airy navies grappling in the central blue;

Far along the world-wide whisper of the south-wind rushing warm,
With the standards of the peoples plunging thro' the thunder-storm;

Till the war-drum throbb'd no longer, and the battle-flags were furl'd
In the Parliament of man, the Federation of the world.

There the common sense of most shall hold a fretful realm in awe,
And the kindly earth shall slumber, lapt in universal law.

So I triumph'd ere my passion sweeping thro' me left me dry,
Left me with the palsied heart, and left me with the jaundiced eye;

Eye, to which all order festers, all things here are out of joint.
Science moves, but slowly, slowly, creeping on from point to point;

Slowly comes a hungry people, as a lion, creeping nigher,
Glares at one that nods and winks behind a slowly-dying fire.

Yet I doubt not thro' the ages one increasing purpose runs,
And the thoughts of men are widen'd with the process of the suns.

What is that to him that reaps not harvest of his youthful joys,
Tho' the deep heart of existence beat for ever like a boy's?

Knowledge comes, but wisdom lingers, and I linger on the shore,
And the individual withers, and the world is more and more.

Knowledge comes, but wisdom lingers, and he bears a laden breast,
Full of sad experience, moving toward the stillness of his rest.

Hark, my merry comrades call me, sounding on the bugle-horn,
They to whom my foolish passion were a target for their scorn.

Shall it not be scorn to me to harp on such a moulder'd string?
I am shamed thro' all my nature to have loved so slight a thing.

Weakness to be wroth with weakness! woman's pleasure, woman's
  pain—
Nature made them blinder motions bounded in a shallower brain.

Woman is the lesser man, and all thy passions, match'd with mine,
Are as moonlight unto sunlight, and as water unto wine—

Here at least, where nature sickens, nothing. Ah, for some retreat
Deep in yonder shining Orient, where my life began to beat,

Where in wild Mahratta-battle fell my father evil-starr'd;—
I was left a trampled orphan, and a selfish uncle's ward.

Or to burst all links of habit—there to wander far away,
On from island unto island at the gateways of the day.

Larger constellations burning, mellow moons and happy skies,
Breadths of tropic shade and palms in cluster, knots of Paradise.

Never comes the trader, never floats an European flag,
Slides the bird o'er lustrous woodland, swings the trailer from the crag;

Droops the heavy-blossom'd bower, hangs the heavy-fruited tree—
Summer isles of Eden lying in dark-purple spheres of sea.

There methinks would be enjoyment more than in this march of mind,
In the steamship, in the railway, in the thoughts that shake mankind.

There the passions cramp'd no longer shall have scope and breathing space;
I will take some savage woman, she shall rear my dusky race.

Iron-jointed, supple-sinew'd, they shall dive, and they shall run,
Catch the wild goat by the hair, and hurl their lances in the sun;

Whistle back the parrot's call, and leap the rainbows of the brooks,
Not with blinded eyesight poring over miserable books—

Fool, again the dream, the fancy! but I *know* my words are wild,
But I count the gray barbarian lower than the Christian child.

I, to herd with narrow foreheads, vacant of our glorious gains,
Like a beast with lower pleasures, like a beast with lower pains!

Mated with a squalid savage—what to me were sun or clime?
I the heir of all the ages, in the foremost files of time—

I that rather held it better men should perish one by one,
Than that earth should stand at gaze like Joshua's moon in Ajalon!

Not in vain the distance beacons. Forward, forward let us range,
Let the great world spin for ever down the ringing grooves of change.

Thro' the shadow of the globe we sweep into the younger day;
Better fifty years of Europe than a cycle of Cathay.

Mother-Age,—for mine I knew not,—help me as when life begun;
Rift the hills, and roll the waters, flash the lightnings, weigh the sun.

O, I see the crescent promise of my spirit hath not set.
Ancient founts of inspiration well thro' all my fancy yet.

Howsoever these things be, a long farewell to Locksley Hall!
Now for me the woods may wither, now for me the roof-tree fall.

Comes a vapor from the margin, blackening over heath and holt,
Cramming all the blast before it, in its breast a thunderbolt.

Let it fall on Locksley Hall, with rain or hail, or fire or snow;
For the mighty wind arises, roaring seaward, and I go.

Saint Agnes' Eve

DEEP on the convent-roof the snows
    Are sparkling to the moon;
My breath to heaven like vapor goes;
    May my soul follow soon!
The shadows of the convent-towers
    Slant down the snowy sward,
Still creeping with the creeping hours
    That lead me to my Lord.
Make Thou my spirit pure and clear
    As are the frosty skies,
Or this first snowdrop of the year
    That in my bosom lies.

As these white robes are soil'd and dark,
    To yonder shining ground;
As this pale taper's earthly spark,
    To yonder argent round;
So shows my soul before the Lamb,
    My spirit before Thee;
So in mine earthly house I am,
    To that I hope to be.
Break up the heavens, O Lord! and far,
    Thro' all yon starlight keen,
Draw me, thy bride, a glittering star,
    In raiment white and clean.

He lifts me to the golden doors;
    The flashes come and go;
All heaven bursts her starry floors,
    And strows her lights below,
And deepens on and up! the gates
    Roll back, and far within
For me the Heavenly Bridegroom waits,
    To make me pure of sin.
The Sabbaths of Eternity,
    One Sabbath deep and wide—
A light upon the shining sea—
    The Bridegroom with his bride!

The Beggar Maid

Her arms across her breast she laid;
  She was more fair than words can say;
Barefooted came the beggar maid
  Before the king Cophetua.
In robe and crown the king stept down,
  To meet and greet her on her way;
'It is no wonder,' said the lords,
  'She is more beautiful than day.'

As shines the moon in clouded skies,
  She in her poor attire was seen;
One praised her ankles, one her eyes,
  One her dark hair and lovesome mien.
So sweet a face, such angel grace,
  In all that land had never been.
Cophetua sware a royal oath:
  'This beggar maid shall be my queen!'

Break, break, break,
  On thy cold gray stones, O Sea!
And I would that my tongue could utter
  The thoughts that arise in me.

O, well for the fisherman's boy,
  That he shouts with his sister at play!
O, well for the sailor lad,
  That he sings in his boat on the bay!

And the stately ships go on
  To their haven under the hill;
But O for the touch of a vanish'd hand,
  And the sound of a voice that is still!

Break, break, break,
  At the foot of thy crags, O Sea!
But the tender grace of a day that is dead
  Will never come back to me.

❧

  SWEET and low, sweet and low,
   Wind of the western sea,
  Low, low, breathe and blow,
   Wind of the western sea !
  Over the rolling waters go,
  Come from the dying moon, and blow,
   Blow him again to me;
While my little one, while my pretty one sleeps.

  Sleep and rest, sleep and rest,
   Father will come to thee soon;
  Rest, rest, on mother's breast,
   Father will come to thee soon;
  Father will come to his babe in the nest,
  Silver sails all out of the west
   Under the silver moon;
Sleep, my little one, sleep, my pretty one, sleep.

❧

  THE splendor falls on castle walls
   And snowy summits old in story;
  The long light shakes across the lakes,
   And the wild cataract leaps in glory.
Blow, bugle, blow, set the wild echoes flying,
Blow, bugle; answer, echoes, dying, dying, dying.

  O, hark, O, hear! how thin and clear,
   And thinner, clearer, farther going !
  O, sweet and far from cliff and scar
   The horns of Elfland faintly blowing !
Blow, let us hear the purple glens replying,
Blow, bugle; answer, echoes, dying, dying, dying.

  O love, they die in yon rich sky,
   They faint on hill or field or river;
  Our echoes roll from soul to soul,
   And grow for ever and for ever.
Blow, bugle, blow, set the wild echoes flying,
And answer, echoes, answer, dying, dying, dying.

❦

   TEARS, idle tears, I know not what they mean,
Tears from the depth of some divine despair
Rise in the heart, and gather to the eyes,
In looking on the happy autumn-fields,
And thinking of the days that are no more.

   Fresh as the first beam glittering on a sail,
That brings our friends up from the underworld,
Sad as the last which reddens over one
That sinks with all we love below the verge;
So sad, so fresh, the days that are no more.

   Ah, sad and strange as in dark summer dawns
The earliest pipe of half-awaken'd birds
To dying ears, when unto dying eyes
The casement slowly grows a glimmering square;
So sad, so strange, the days that are no more.

   Dear as remember'd kisses after death,
And sweet as those by hopeless fancy feign'd
On lips that are for others; deep as love,
Deep as first love, and wild with all regret;
O Death in Life, the days that are no more!

❦

   O SWALLOW, Swallow, flying, flying south,
Fly to her, and fall upon her gilded eaves,
And tell her, tell her, what I tell to thee.

   O, tell her, Swallow, thou that knowest each,
That bright and fierce and fickle is the South,
And dark and true and tender is the North.

   O Swallow, Swallow, if I could follow, and light
Upon her lattice, I would pipe and trill,
And cheep and twitter twenty million loves.

   O, were I thou that she might take me in,
And lay me on her bosom, and her heart
Would rock the snowy cradle till I died!

Why lingereth she to clothe her heart with love,
Delaying as the tender ash delays
To clothe herself, when all the woods are green?

O, tell her, Swallow, that thy brood is flown;
Say to her, I do but wanton in the South,
But in the North long since my nest is made.

O, tell her, brief is life but love is long,
And brief the sun of summer in the North,
And brief the moon of beauty in the South.

O Swallow, flying from the golden woods,
Fly to her, and pipe and woo her, and make her mine,
And tell her, tell her, that I follow thee.

      ᶻ●

HOME they brought her warrior dead;
   She nor swoon'd nor utter'd cry.
All her maidens, watching, said,
   'She must weep or she will die.'

Then they praised him, soft and low,
   Call'd him worthy to be loved,
Truest friend and noblest foe;
   Yet she neither spoke nor moved.

Stole a maiden from her place,
   Lightly to the warrior stept,
Took the face-cloth from the face;
   Yet she neither moved nor wept.

Rose a nurse of ninety years,
   Set his child upon her knee—
Like summer tempest came her tears—
   'Sweet my child, I live for thee.'

      ᶻ●

NOW sleeps the crimson petal, now the white;
Nor waves the cypress in the palace walk;
Nor winks the gold fin in the porphyry font.
The fire-fly wakens; waken thou with me.

Now droops the milk-white peacock like a ghost,
And like a ghost she glimmers on to me.

Now lies the Earth all Danaë to the stars,
And all thy heart lies open unto me.

Now slides the silent meteor on, and leaves
A shining furrow, as thy thoughts in me.

Now folds the lily all her sweetness up,
And slips into the bosom of the lake.
So fold thyself, my dearest, thou, and slip
Into my bosom and be lost in me.

&

COME down, O maid, from yonder mountain height.
What pleasure lives in height (the shepherd sang),
In height and cold, the splendor of the hills?
But cease to move so near the heavens, and cease
To glide a sunbeam by the blasted pine,
To sit a star upon the sparkling spire;
And come, for Love is of the valley, come,
For Love is of the valley, come thou down
And find him; by the happy threshold, he,
Or hand in hand with Plenty in the maize,
Or red with spirted purple of the vats,
Or foxlike in the vine; nor cares to walk
With Death and Morning on the Silver Horns,
Nor wilt thou snare him in the white ravine,
Nor find him dropt upon the firths of ice,
That huddling slant in furrow-cloven falls
To roll the torrent out of dusky doors.
But follow; let the torrent dance thee down
To find him in the valley; let the wild
Lean-headed eagles yelp alone, and leave
The monstrous ledges there to slope, and spill
Their thousand wreaths of dangling water-smoke,
That like a broken purpose waste in air.
So waste not thou, but come; for all the vales
Await thee; azure pillars of the hearth
Arise to thee; the children call, and I

Thy shepherd pipe, and sweet is every sound,
Sweeter thy voice, but every sound is sweet;
Myriads of rivulets hurrying thro' the lawn,
The moan of doves in immemorial elms,
And murmuring of innumerable bees.

I

COME into the garden, Maud,
   For the black bat, night, has flown,
Come into the garden, Maud,
   I am here at the gate alone;
And the woodbine spices are wafted abroad,
   And the musk of the rose is blown.

II

For a breeze of morning moves,
   And the planet of Love is on high,
Beginning to faint in the light that she loves
   On a bed of daffodil sky,
To faint in the light of the sun she loves,
   To faint in his light, and to die.

III

All night have the roses heard
   The flute, violin, bassoon:
All night has the casement jessamine stirr'd
   To the dancers dancing in tune;
Till a silence fell with the waking bird,
   And a hush with the setting moon.

IV

I said to the lily, 'There is but one,
   With whom she has heart to be gay.
When will the dancers leave her alone?
   She is weary of dance and play.'

Now half to the setting moon are gone,
    And half to the rising day;
Low on the sand and loud on the stone
    The last wheel echoes away.

V

I said to the rose, 'The brief night goes
    In babble and revel and wine.
O young lord-lover, what sighs are those,
    For one that will never be thine?
But mine, but mine,' so I sware to the rose,
    'For ever and ever, mine.'

VI

And the soul of the rose went into my blood,
    As the music clash'd in the hall;
And long by the garden lake I stood,
    For I heard your rivulet fall
From the lake to the meadow and on to the wood,
    Our wood, that is dearer than all;

VII

From the meadow your walks have left so sweet
    That whenever a March-wind sighs
He sets the jewel-print of your feet
    In violets blue as your eyes,
To the woody hollows in which we meet
    And the valleys of Paradise.

VIII

The slender acacia would not shake
    One long milk-bloom on the tree;
The white lake-blossom fell into the lake
    As the pimpernel dozed on the lea;
But the rose was awake all night for your sake,
    Knowing your promise to me;
The lilies and roses were all awake,
    They sigh'd for the dawn and thee.

IX

Queen rose of the rosebud garden of girls,
   Come hither, the dances are done,
In gloss of satin and glimmer of pearls,
   Queen lily and rose in one;
Shine out, little head, sunning over with curls,
   To the flowers, and be their sun.

X

There has fallen a splendid tear
   From the passion-flower at the gate.
She is coming, my dove, my dear;
   She is coming, my life, my fate.
The red rose cries, 'She is near, she is near;'
   And the white rose weeps, 'She is late;'
The larkspur listens, 'I hear, I hear;'
   And the lily whispers, 'I wait.'

XI

She is coming, my own, my sweet;
   Were it ever so airy a tread,
My heart would hear her and beat,
   Were it earth in an earthy bed;
My dust would hear her and beat,
   Had I lain for a century dead,
Would start and tremble under her feet,
   And blossom in purple and red.

The Song of the Brook

I COME from haunts of coot and hern,
   I make a sudden sally,
And sparkle out among the fern,
   To bicker down a valley.

By thirty hills I hurry down,
   Or slip between the ridges,
By twenty thorps, a little town,
   And half a hundred bridges.

Till last by Philip's farm I flow
   To join the brimming river,
For men may come and men may go,
   But I go on for ever.

I chatter over stony ways,
   In little sharps and trebles,
I bubble into eddying bays,
   I babble on the pebbles.

With many a curve my banks I fret
   By many a field and fallow,
And many a fairy foreland set
   With willow-weed and mallow.

I chatter, chatter, as I flow
   To join the brimming river,
For men may come and men may go,
   But I go on for ever.

I wind about, and in and out,
   With here a blossom sailing,
And here and there a lusty trout,
   And here and there a grayling,

And here and there a foamy flake
   Upon me, as I travel
With many a silvery water-break
   Above the golden gravel,

And draw them all along, and flow
   To join the brimming river,
For men may come and men may go,
   But I go on for ever.

Ode on the Death of the Duke of Wellington

I

BURY the Great Duke
   With an empire's lamentation;
Let us bury the Great Duke
   To the noise of the mourning of a mighty nation;
Mourning when their leaders fall,

Warriors carry the warrior's pall,
And sorrow darkens hamlet and hall.

II

Where shall we lay the man whom we deplore?
Here, in streaming London's central roar.
Let the sound of those he wrought for,
And the feet of those he fought for,
Echo round his bones for evermore.

III

Lead out the pageant: sad and slow,
As fits an universal woe,
Let the long, long procession go,
And let the sorrowing crowd about it grow,
And let the mournful martial music blow;
The last great Englishman is low.

IV

Mourn, for to us he seems the last,
Remembering all his greatness in the past.
No more in soldier fashion will he greet
With lifted hand the gazer in the street.
O friends, our chief state-oracle is mute!
Mourn for the man of long-enduring blood,
The statesman-warrior, moderate, resolute,
Whole in himself, a common good.
Mourn for the man of amplest influence,
Yet clearest of ambitious crime,
Our greatest yet with least pretence,
Great in council and great in war,
Foremost captain of his time,
Rich in saving common-sense,
And, as the greatest only are,
In his simplicity sublime.
O good gray head which all men knew,
O voice from which their omens all men drew,
O iron nerve to true occasion true,
O fallen at length that tower of strength
Which stood four-square to all the winds that blew!

Such was he whom we deplore.
The long self-sacrifice of life is o'er.
The great World-victor's victor will be seen no more.

V

All is over and done.
Render thanks to the Giver,
England, for thy son.
Let the bell be toll'd.
Render thanks to the Giver,
And render him to the mould.
Under the cross of gold
That shines over city and river,
There he shall rest for ever
Among the wise and the bold.
Let the bell be toll'd,
And a reverent people behold
The towering car, the sable steeds.
Bright let it be with its blazon'd deeds,
Dark in its funeral fold.
Let the bell be toll'd,
And a deeper knell in the heart be knoll'd;
And the sound of the sorrowing anthem roll'd
Thro' the dome of the golden cross;
And the volleying cannon thunder his loss;
He knew their voices of old.
For many a time in many a clime
His captain's-ear has heard them boom
Bellowing victory, bellowing doom.
When he with those deep voices wrought,
Guarding realms and kings from shame,
With those deep voices our dead captain taught
The tyrant, and asserts his claim
In that dread sound to the great name
Which he has worn so pure of blame,
In praise and in dispraise the same,
A man of well-attemper'd frame.
O civic muse, to such a name,
To such a name for ages long,
To such a name,
Preserve a broad approach of fame,
And ever-echoing avenues of song!

VI

'Who is he that cometh, like an honor'd guest,
With banner and with music, with soldier and with priest,
With a nation weeping, and breaking on my rest?'—
Mighty Seaman, this is he
Was great by land as thou by sea.
Thine island loves thee well, thou famous man,
The greatest sailor since our world began.
Now, to the roll of muffled drums,
To thee the greatest soldier comes;
For this is he
Was great by land as thou by sea.
His foes were thine; he kept us free;
O, give him welcome, this is he
Worthy of our gorgeous rites,
And worthy to be laid by thee;
For this is England's greatest son,
He that gain'd a hundred fights,
Nor ever lost an English gun;
This is he that far away
Against the myriads of Assaye
Clash'd with his fiery few and won;
And underneath another sun,
Warring on a later day,
Round affrighted Lisbon drew
The treble works, the vast designs
Of his labor'd rampart-lines,
Where he greatly stood at bay,
Whence he issued forth anew,
And ever great and greater grew,
Beating from the wasted vines
Back to France her banded swarms,
Back to France with countless blows,
Till o'er the hills her eagles flew
Beyond the Pyrenean pines,
Follow'd up in valley and glen
With blare of bugle, clamor of men,
Roll of cannon and clash of arms,
And England pouring on her foes.
Such a war had such a close.
Again their ravening eagle rose

In anger, wheel'd on Europe-shadowing wings,
And barking for the thrones of kings;
Till one that sought but Duty's iron crown
On that loud Sabbath shook the spoiler down;
A day of onsets of despair!
Dash'd on every rocky square,
Their surging charges foam'd themselves away;
Last, the Prussian trumpet blew;
Thro' the long-tormented air
Heaven flash'd a sudden jubilant ray,
And down we swept and charged and overthrew.
So great a soldier taught us there
What long-enduring hearts could do
In that world-earthquake, Waterloo!
Mighty Seaman, tender and true,
And pure as he from taint of craven guile,
O saviour of the silver-coasted isle,
O shaker of the Baltic and the Nile,
If aught of things that here befall
Touch a spirit among things divine,
If love of country move thee there at all,
Be glad, because his bones are laid by thine,
And thro' the centuries let a people's voice
In full acclaim,
A people's voice,
The proof and echo of all human fame,
A people's voice, when they rejoice
At civic revel and pomp and game,
Attest their great commander's claim
With honor, honor, honor, honor to him,
Eternal honor to his name.

VII

A people's voice! we are a people yet.
Tho' all men else their nobler dreams forget,
Confused by brainless mobs and lawless Powers,
Thank Him who isled us here, and roughly set
His Briton in blown seas and storming showers,
We have a voice with which to pay the debt
Of boundless love and reverence and regret
To those great men who fought, and kept it ours.

And keep it ours, O God, from brute control!
O Statesmen, guard us, guard the eye, the soul
Of Europe, keep our noble England whole,
And save the one true seed of freedom sown
Betwixt a people and their ancient throne,
That sober freedom out of which there springs
Our loyal passion for our temperate kings!
For, saving that, ye help to save mankind
Till public wrong be crumbled into dust,
And drill the raw world for the march of mind,
Till crowds at length be sane and crowns be just.
But wink no more in slothful overtrust.
Remember him who led your hosts;
He bade you guard the sacred coasts.
Your cannons moulder on the seaward wall;
His voice is silent in your council-hall
For ever; and whatever tempests lour
For ever silent; even if they broke
In thunder, silent; yet remember all
He spoke among you, and the Man who spoke;
Who never sold the truth to serve the hour,
Nor palter'd with Eternal God for power;
Who let the turbid streams of rumor flow
Thro' either babbling world of high and low;
Whose life was work, whose language rife
With rugged maxims hewn from life;
Who never spoke against a foe;
Whose eighty winters freeze with one rebuke
All great self-seekers trampling on the right.
Truth-teller was our England's Alfred named;
Truth-lover was our English Duke;
Whatever record leap to light
He never shall be shamed.

VIII

Lo! the leader in these glorious wars
Now to glorious burial slowly borne,
Follow'd by the brave of other lands,
He, on whom from both her open hands
Lavish Honor shower'd all her stars,
And affluent Fortune emptied all her horn.
Yea, let all good things await

Him who cares not to be great
But as he saves or serves the state.
Not once or twice in our rough island-story
The path of duty was the way to glory.
He that walks it, only thirsting
For the right, and learns to deaden
Love of self, before his journey closes,
He shall find the stubborn thistle bursting
Into glossy purples, which outredden
All voluptuous garden-roses.
Not once or twice in our fair island-story
The path of duty was the way to glory.
He, that ever following her commands,
On with toil of heart and knees and hands,
Thro' the long gorge to the far light has won
His path upward, and prevail'd,
Shall find the toppling crags of Duty scaled
Are close upon the shining table-lands
To which our God Himself is moon and sun.
Such was he: his work is done.
But while the races of mankind endure
Let his great example stand
Colossal, seen of every land,
And keep the soldier firm, the statesman pure;
Till in all lands and thro' all human story
The path of duty be the way to glory.
And let the land whose hearths he saved from shame
For many and many an age proclaim
At civic revel and pomp and game,
And when the long-illumined cities flame,
Their ever-loyal iron leader's fame,
With honor, honor, honor, honor to him,
Eternal honor to his name.

IX

Peace, his triumph will be sung
By some yet unmoulded tongue
Far on in summers that we shall not see.
Peace, it is a day of pain
For one about whose patriarchal knee
Late the little children clung.
O peace, it is a day of pain
For one upon whose hand and heart and brain

Once the weight and fate of Europe hung.
Ours the pain, be his the gain!
More than is of man's degree
Must be with us, watching here
At this, our great solemnity.
Whom we see not we revere;
We revere, and we refrain
From talk of battles loud and vain,
And brawling memories all too free
For such a wise humility
As befits a solemn fane:
We revere, and while we hear
The tides of Music's golden sea
Setting toward eternity,
Uplifted high in heart and hope are we,
Until we doubt not that for one so true
There must be other nobler work to do
Than when he fought at Waterloo,
And Victor he must ever be.
For tho' the Giant Ages heave the hill
And break the shore, and evermore
Make and break, and work their will,
Tho' world on world in myriad myriads roll
Round us, each with different powers,
And other forms of life than ours,
What know we greater than the soul?
On God and Godlike men we build our trust.
Hush, the Dead March wails in the people's ears;
The dark crowd moves, and there are sobs and tears;
The black earth yawns; the mortal disappears;
Ashes to ashes, dust to dust;
He is gone who seem'd so great.—
Gone, but nothing can bereave him
Of the force he made his own
Being here, and we believe him
Something far advanced in State,
And that he wears a truer crown
Than any wreath that man can weave him.
Speak no more of his renown,
Lay your earthly fancies down,
And in the vast cathedral leave him,
God accept him, Christ receive him!
   1852.

The Charge of the Light Brigade

I

Half a league, half a league,
Half a league onward,
All in the valley of Death
   Rode the six hundred.
'Forward the Light Brigade !
Charge for the guns !' he said.
Into the valley of Death
   Rode the six hundred.

II

'Forward, the Light Brigade !'
Was there a man dismay'd ?
Not tho' the soldier knew
   Some one had blunder'd.
Theirs not to make reply,
Theirs not to reason why,
Theirs but to do and die.
Into the valley of Death
   Rode the six hundred.

III

Cannon to right of them,
Cannon to left of them,
Cannon in front of them
   Volley'd and thunder'd;
Storm'd at with shot and shell,
Boldly they rode and well,
Into the jaws of Death,
Into the mouth of hell
   Rode the six hundred.

IV

Flash'd all their sabres bare,
Flash'd as they turn'd in air
Sabring the gunners there,
Charging an army, while
   All the world wonder'd.

Plunged in the battery-smoke
Right thro' the line they broke;
Cossack and Russian
Reel'd from the sabre-stroke
   Shatter'd and sunder'd.
Then they rode back, but not,
   Not the six hundred.

V

Cannon to right of them,
Cannon to left of them,
Cannon behind them
   Volley'd and thunder'd;
Storm'd at with shot and shell,
While horse and hero fell,
They that had fought so well
Came thro' the jaws of Death,
Back from the mouth of hell,
All that was left of them,
   Left of six hundred.

VI

When can their glory fade?
O the wild charge they made!
   All the world wonder'd.
Honor the charge they made!
Honor the Light Brigade,
   Noble six hundred!

Enoch Arden

   LONG lines of cliff breaking have left a chasm;
And in the chasm are foam and yellow sands;
Beyond, red roofs about a narrow wharf
In cluster; then a moulder'd church; and higher
A long street climbs to one tall-tower'd mill;
And high in heaven behind it a gray down
With Danish barrows; and a hazel-wood,
By autumn nutters haunted, flourishes
Green in a cuplike hollow of the down.

Here on this beach a hundred years ago,
Three children of three houses, Annie Lee,
The prettiest little damsel in the port,
And Philip Ray, the miller's only son,
And Enoch Arden, a rough sailor's lad
Made orphan by a winter shipwreck, play'd
Among the waste and lumber of the shore,
Hard coils of cordage, swarthy fishing-nets,
Anchors of rusty fluke, and boats updrawn;
And built their castles of dissolving sand
To watch them overflow'd, or following up
And flying the white breaker, daily left
The little footprint daily wash'd away.

A narrow cave ran in beneath the cliff;
In this the children play'd at keeping house.
Enoch was host one day, Philip the next,
While Annie still was mistress; but at times
Enoch would hold possession for a week:
'This is my house and this my little wife.'
'Mine too,' said Philip; 'turn and turn about;'
When, if they quarrell'd, Enoch stronger-made
Was master. Then would Philip, his blue eyes
All flooded with the helpless wrath of tears,
Shriek out, 'I hate you, Enoch,' and at this
The little wife would weep for company,
And pray them not to quarrel for her sake,
And say she would be little wife to both.

But when the dawn of rosy childhood past,
And the new warmth of life's ascending sun
Was felt by either, either fixt his heart
On that one girl; and Enoch spoke his love,
But Philip loved in silence; and the girl
Seem'd kinder unto Philip than to him;
But she loved Enoch, tho' she knew it not,
And would if ask'd deny it. Enoch set
A purpose evermore before his eyes,
To hoard all savings to the uttermost,
To purchase his own boat, and make a home
For Annie; and so prosper'd that at last
A luckier or a bolder fisherman,
A carefuller in peril, did not breathe
For leagues along that breaker-beaten coast

Than Enoch. Likewise had he served a year
On board a merchantman, and made himself
Full sailor; and he thrice had pluck'd a life
From the dread sweep of the down-streaming seas,
And all men look'd upon him favorably.
And ere he touch'd his one-and-twentieth May
He purchased his own boat, and made a home
For Annie, neat and nestlike, halfway up
The narrow street that clamber'd toward the mill.

   Then, on a golden autumn eventide,
The younger people making holiday,
With bag and sack and basket, great and small,
Went nutting to the hazels. Philip stay'd—
His father lying sick and needing him—
An hour behind; but as he climb'd the hill,
Just where the prone edge of the wood began
To feather toward the hollow, saw the pair,
Enoch and Annie, sitting hand-in-hand,
His large gray eyes and weather-beaten face
All-kindled by a still and sacred fire,
That burn'd as on an altar. Philip look'd,
And in their eyes and faces read his doom;
Then, as their faces drew together, groan'd,
And slipt aside, and like a wounded life
Crept down into the hollows of the wood;
There, while the rest were loud in merrymaking,
Had his dark hour unseen, and rose and past
Bearing a lifelong hunger in his heart.

   So these were wed, and merrily rang the bells,
And merrily ran the years, seven happy years,
Seven happy years of health and competence,
And mutual love and honorable toil,
With children, first a daughter. In him woke,
With his first babe's first cry, the noble wish
To save all earnings to the uttermost,
And give his child a better bringing-up
Than his had been, or hers; a wish renew'd,
When two years after came a boy to be
The rosy idol of her solitudes,
While Enoch was abroad on wrathful seas,
Or often journeying landward; for in truth
Enoch's white horse, and Enoch's ocean-spoil

In ocean-smelling osier, and his face,
Rough-redden'd with a thousand winter gales,
Not only to the market-cross were known,
But in the leafy lanes behind the down,
Far as the portal-warding lion-whelp
And peacock yew-tree of the lonely Hall,
Whose Friday fare was Enoch's ministering.

   Then came a change, as all things human change.
Ten miles to northward of the narrow port
Open'd a larger haven. Thither used
Enoch at times to go by land or sea;
And once when there, and clambering on a mast
In harbor, by mischance he slipt and fell.
A limb was broken when they lifted him;
And while he lay recovering there, his wife
Bore him another son, a sickly one.
Another hand crept too across his trade
Taking her bread and theirs; and on him fell,
Altho' a grave and staid God-fearing man,
Yet lying thus inactive, doubt and gloom.
He seem'd, as in a nightmare of the night,
To see his children leading evermore
Low miserable lives of hand-to-mouth,
And her he loved a beggar. Then he pray'd,
'Save them from this, whatever comes to me.'
And while he pray'd, the master of that ship
Enoch had served in, hearing his mischance,
Came, for he knew the man and valued him,
Reporting of his vessel China-bound,
And wanting yet a boatswain. Would he go?
There yet were many weeks before she sail'd,
Sail'd from this port. Would Enoch have the place?
And Enoch all at once assented to it,
Rejoicing at that answer to his prayer.

   So now that shadow of mischance appear'd
No graver than as when some little cloud
Cuts off the fiery highway of the sun,
And isles a light in the offing. Yet the wife—
When he was gone—the children—what to do?
Then Enoch lay long-pondering on his plans:
To sell the boat—and yet he loved her well—
How many a rough sea had he weather'd in her!

He knew her, as a horseman knows his horse—
And yet to sell her—then with what she brought
Buy goods and stores—set Annie forth in trade
With all that seamen needed or their wives—
So might she keep the house while he was gone.
Should he not trade himself out yonder? go
This voyage more than once? yea, twice or thrice—
As oft as needed—last, returning rich,
Become the master of a larger craft,
With fuller profits lead an easier life,
Have all his pretty young ones educated,
And pass his days in peace among his own.

   Thus Enoch in his heart determined all;
Then moving homeward came on Annie pale,
Nursing the sickly babe, her latest-born.
Forward she started with a happy cry,
And laid the feeble infant in his arms;
Whom Enoch took, and handled all his limbs,
Appraised his weight and fondled father-like,
But had no heart to break his purposes
To Annie, till the morrow, when he spoke.

   Then first since Enoch's golden ring had girt
Her finger, Annie fought against his will;
Yet not with brawling opposition she,
But manifold entreaties, many a tear,
Many a sad kiss by day, by night, renew'd—
Sure that all evil would come out of it—
Besought him, supplicating, if he cared
For her or his dear children, not to go.
He not for his own self caring, but her,
Her and her children, let her plead in vain;
So grieving held his will, and bore it thro'.

   For Enoch parted with his old sea-friend,
Bought Annie goods and stores, and set his hand
To fit their little streetward sitting-room
With shelf and corner for the goods and stores.
So all day long till Enoch's last at home,
Shaking their pretty cabin, hammer and axe,
Auger and saw, while Annie seem'd to hear
Her own death-scaffold raising, shrill'd and rang,
Till this was ended, and his careful hand,—

The space was narrow,—having order'd all
Almost as neat and close as Nature packs
Her blossom or her seedling, paused; and he,
Who needs would work for Annie to the last,
Ascending tired, heavily slept till morn.

And Enoch faced this morning of farewell
Brightly and boldly. All his Annie's fears,
Save as his Annie's, were a laughter to him.
Yet Enoch as a brave God-fearing man
Bow'd himself down, and in that mystery
Where God-in-man is one with man-in-God,
Pray'd for a blessing on his wife and babes,
Whatever came to him; and then he said:
'Annie, this voyage by the grace of God
Will bring fair weather yet to all of us.
Keep a clean hearth and a clear fire for me,
For I'll be back, my girl, before you know it;'
Then lightly rocking baby's cradle, 'and he,
This pretty, puny, weakly little one,—
Nay—for I love him all the better for it—
God bless him, he shall sit upon my knees
And I will tell him tales of foreign parts,
And make him merry, when I come home again.
Come, Annie, come, cheer up before I go.'

Him running on thus hopefully she heard,
And almost hoped herself; but when he turn'd
The current of his talk to graver things
In sailor fashion roughly sermonizing
On providence and trust in heaven, she heard,
Heard and not heard him; as the village girl,
Who sets her pitcher underneath the spring,
Musing on him that used to fill it for her,
Hears and not hears, and lets it overflow.

At length she spoke: 'O Enoch, you are wise;
And yet for all your wisdom well know I
That I shall look upon your face no more.'

'Well, then,' said Enoch, 'I shall look on yours.
Annie, the ship I sail in passes here'—
He named the day;—'get you a seaman's glass,
Spy out my face, and laugh at all your fears.'

But when the last of those last moments came:
'Annie, my girl, cheer up, be comforted,
Look to the babes, and till I come again
Keep everything shipshape, for I must go.
And fear no more for me; or if you fear,
Cast all your cares on God; that anchor holds.
Is He not yonder in those uttermost
Parts of the morning? if I flee to these,
Can I go from Him? and the sea is His,
The sea is His; He made it.'

                                        Enoch rose,
Cast his strong arms about his drooping wife,
And kiss'd his wonder-stricken little ones;
But for the third, the sickly one, who slept
After a night of feverous wakefulness,
When Annie would have raised him Enoch said,
'Wake him not, let him sleep; how should the child
Remember this?' and kiss'd him in his cot.
But Annie from her baby's forehead clipt
A tiny curl, and gave it; this he kept
Thro' all his future, but now hastily caught
His bundle, waved his hand, and went his way.

   She, when the day that Enoch mention'd came,
Borrow'd a glass, but all in vain. Perhaps
She could not fix the glass to suit her eye;
Perhaps her eye was dim, hand tremulous;
She saw him not, and while he stood on deck
Waving, the moment and the vessel past.

   Even to the last dip of the vanishing sail
She watch'd it, and departed weeping for him;
Then, tho' she mourn'd his absence as his grave,
Set her sad will no less to chime with his,
But throve not in her trade, not being bred
To barter, nor compensating the want
By shrewdness, neither capable of lies,
Nor asking overmuch and taking less,
And still foreboding 'what would Enoch say?'
For more than once, in days of difficulty
And pressure, had she sold her wares for less
Than what she gave in buying what she sold.

She fail'd and sadden'd knowing it; and thus,
Expectant of that news which never came,
Gain'd for her own a scanty sustenance,
And lived a life of silent melancholy.

Now the third child was sickly-born and grew
Yet sicklier, tho' the mother cared for it
With all a mother's care; nevertheless,
Whether her business often call'd her from it,
Or thro' the want of what it needed most,
Or means to pay the voice who best could tell
What most it needed—howsoe'er it was,
After a lingering,—ere she was aware,—
Like the caged bird escaping suddenly,
The little innocent soul flitted away.

In that same week when Annie buried it,
Philip's true heart, which hunger'd for her peace,—
Since Enoch left he had not look'd upon her,—
Smote him, as having kept aloof so long.
'Surely,' said Philip, 'I may see her now,
May be some little comfort;' therefore went,
Past thro' the solitary room in front,
Paused for a moment at an inner door,
Then struck it thrice, and, no one opening,
Enter'd, but Annie, seated with her grief,
Fresh from the burial of her little one,
Cared not to look on any human face,
But turn'd her own toward the wall and wept.
Then Philip standing up said falteringly,
'Annie, I came to ask a favor of you.'

He spoke; the passion in her moan'd reply,
'Favor from one so sad and so forlorn
As I am!' half abash'd him; yet unask'd,
His bashfulness and tenderness at war,
He set himself beside her, saying to her:

'I came to speak to you of what he wish'd,
Enoch, your husband. I have ever said
You chose the best among us—a strong man;
For where he fixt his heart he set his hand
To do the thing he will'd, and bore it thro'.
And wherefore did he go this weary way,
And leave you lonely? not to see the world—

For pleasure?—nay, but for the wherewithal
To give his babes a better bringing up
Than his had been, or yours; that was his wish.
And if he come again, vext will he be
To find the precious morning hours were lost.
And it would vex him even in his grave,
If he could know his babes were running wild
Like colts about the waste. So, Annie, now—
Have we not known each other all our lives?
I do beseech you by the love you bear
Him and his children not to say me nay—
For, if you will, when Enoch comes again
Why then he shall repay me—if you will,
Annie—for I am rich and well-to-do.
Now let me put the boy and girl to school;
This is the favor that I came to ask.'

    Then Annie with her brows against the wall
Answer'd, 'I cannot look you in the face;
I seem so foolish and so broken down.
When you came in my sorrow broke me down;
And now I think your kindness breaks me down.
But Enoch lives; that is borne in on me;
He will repay you. Money can be repaid,
Not kindness such as yours.'
                            And Philip ask'd,
'Then you will let me, Annie?'
                                    There she turn'd,
She rose, and fixt her swimming eyes upon him,
And dwelt a moment on his kindly face,
Then calling down a blessing on his head
Caught at his hand, and wrung it passionately,
And past into the little garth beyond.
So lifted up in spirit he moved away.

    Then Philip put the boy and girl to school,
And bought them needful books, and every way,
Like one who does his duty by his own,
Made himself theirs; and tho' for Annie's sake,
Fearing the lazy gossip of the port,
He oft denied his heart his dearest wish,
And seldom crost her threshold, yet he sent
Gifts by the children, garden-herbs and fruit,

The late and early roses from his wall,
Or conies from the down, and now and then,
With some pretext of fineness in the meal
To save the offence of charitable, flour
From his tall mill that whistled on the waste.

But Philip did not fathom Annie's mind;
Scarce could the woman, when he came upon her,
Out of full heart and boundless gratitude
Light on a broken word to thank him with.
But Philip was her children's all-in-all;
From distant corners of the street they ran
To greet his hearty welcome heartily;
Lords of his house and of his mill were they,
Worried his passive ear with petty wrongs
Or pleasures, hung upon him, play'd with him
And call'd him Father Philip. Philip gain'd
As Enoch lost, for Enoch seem'd to them
Uncertain as a vision or a dream,
Faint as a figure seen in early dawn
Down at the far end of an avenue,
Going we know not where; and so ten years,
Since Enoch left his hearth and native land,
Fled forward, and no news of Enoch came.

It chanced one evening Annie's children long'd
To go with others nutting to the wood,
And Annie would go with them; then they begg'd
For Father Philip, as they call'd him, too.
Him, like the working bee in blossom-dust,
Blanch'd with his mill, they found; and saying to him,
'Come with us, Father Philip,' he denied;
But when the children pluck'd at him to go,
He laugh'd, and yielded readily to their wish,
For was not Annie with them ? and they went.

But after scaling half the weary down,
Just where the prone edge of the wood began
To feather toward the hollow, all her force
Fail'd her; and sighing, 'Let me rest,' she said.
So Philip rested with her well-content;
While all the younger ones with jubilant cries
Broke from their elders, and tumultuously
Down thro' the whitening hazels made a plunge

To the bottom, and dispersed, and bent or broke
The lithe reluctant boughs to tear away
Their tawny clusters, crying to each other
And calling, here and there, about the wood.

    But Philip sitting at her side forgot
Her presence, and remember'd one dark hour
Here in this wood, when like a wounded life
He crept into the shadow. At last he said,
Lifting his honest forehead, 'Listen, Annie,
How merry they are down yonder in the wood.
Tired, Annie?' for she did not speak a word.
'Tired?' but her face had fallen upon her hands;
At which, as with a kind of anger in him,
'The ship was lost,' he said, 'the ship was lost!
No more of that! why should you kill yourself
And make them orphans quite?' And Annie said,
'I thought not of it; but—I know not why—
Their voices make me feel so solitary.'

    Then Philip coming somewhat closer spoke:
'Annie, there is a thing upon my mind,
And it has been upon my mind so long
That, tho' I know not when it first came there,
I know that it will out at last. O Annie,
It is beyond all hope, against all chance,
That he who left you ten long years ago
Should still be living; well, then—let me speak.
I grieve to see you poor and wanting help;
I cannot help you as I wish to do
Unless—they say that women are so quick—
Perhaps you know what I would have you know—
I wish you for my wife. I fain would prove
A father to your children; I do think
They love me as a father; I am sure
That I love them as if they were mine own;
And I believe, if you were fast my wife,
That after all these sad uncertain years
We might be still as happy as God grants
To any of his creatures. Think upon it;
For I am well-to-do—no kin, no care,
No burthen, save my care for you and yours,
And we have known each other all our lives,
And I have loved you longer than you know.'

Then answer'd Annie—tenderly she spoke:
'You have been as God's good angel in our house.
God bless you for it, God reward you for it,
Philip, with something happier than myself.
Can one love twice ? can you be ever loved
As Enoch was ? what is it that you ask ?'
'I am content,' he answer'd, 'to be loved
A little after Enoch.' 'O,' she cried,
Scared as it were, 'dear Philip, wait a while.
If Enoch comes—but Enoch will not come—
Yet wait a year, a year is not so long.
Surely I shall be wiser in a year.
O, wait a little !' Philip sadly said,
'Annie, as I have waited all my life
I well may wait a little.' 'Nay,' she cried,
'I am bound: you have my promise—in a year.
Will you not bide your year as I bide mine ?'
And Philip answer'd, 'I will bide my year.'

Here both were mute, till Philip glancing up
Beheld the dead flame of the fallen day
Pass from the Danish barrow overhead;
Then, fearing night and chill for Annie, rose
And sent his voice beneath him thro' the wood.
Up came the children laden with their spoil;
Then all descended to the port, and there
At Annie's door he paused and gave his hand,
Saying gently, 'Annie, when I spoke to you,
That was your hour of weakness. I was wrong,
I am always bound to you, but you are free.'
Then Annie weeping answer'd, 'I am bound.'

She spoke; and in one moment as it were,
While yet she went about her household ways,
Even as she dwelt upon his latest words,
That he had loved her longer than she knew,
That autumn into autumn flash'd again,
And there he stood once more before her face,
Claiming her promise. 'Is it a year ?' she ask'd.
'Yes, if the nuts,' he said, 'be ripe again;
Come out and see.' But she—she put him off—
So much to look to—such a change—a month—

Give her a month—she knew that she was bound—
A month—no more. Then Philip with his eyes
Full of that lifelong hunger, and his voice
Shaking a little like a drunkard's hand,
'Take your own time, Annie, take your own time.'
And Annie could have wept for pity of him;
And yet she held him on delayingly
With many a scarce-believable excuse,
Trying his truth and his long-sufferance,
Till half another year had slipt away.

   By this the lazy gossips of the port,
Abhorrent of a calculation crost,
Began to chafe as at a personal wrong.
Some thought that Philip did but trifle with her;
Some that she but held off to draw him on;
And others laugh'd at her and Philip too,
As simple folk that knew not their own minds;
And one, in whom all evil fancies clung
Like serpent eggs together, laughingly
Would hint at worse in either. Her own son
Was silent, tho' he often look'd his wish;
But evermore the daughter prest upon her
To wed the man so dear to all of them
And lift the household out of poverty;
And Philip's rosy face contracting grew
Careworn and wan; and all these things fell on her
Sharp as reproach.

               At last one night it chanced
That Annie could not sleep, but earnestly
Pray'd for a sign, 'My Enoch, is he gone?'
Then compass'd round by the blind wall of night
Brook'd not the expectant terror of her heart,
Started from bed, and struck herself a light,
Then desperately seized the holy Book,
Suddenly set it wide to find a sign,
Suddenly put her finger on the text,
'Under the palm-tree.' That was nothing to her,
No meaning there; she closed the Book and slept.
When lo! her Enoch sitting on a height,
Under a palm-tree, over him the sun.
'He is gone,' she thought, 'he is happy, he is singing

Hosanna in the highest; yonder shines
The Sun of Righteousness, and these be palms
Whereof the happy people strowing cried
"Hosanna in the highest!" ' Here she woke,
Resolved, sent for him and said wildly to him,
'There is no reason why we should not wed.'
'Then for God's sake,' he answer'd, 'both our sakes,
So you will wed me, let it be at once.'

   So these were wed, and merrily rang the bells,
Merrily rang the bells, and they were wed.
But never merrily beat Annie's heart.
A footstep seem'd to fall beside her path,
She knew not whence; a whisper on her ear,
She knew not what; nor loved she to be left
Alone at home, nor ventured out alone.
What ail'd her then that, ere she enter'd, often
Her hand dwelt lingeringly on the latch,
Fearing to enter? Philip thought he knew:
Such doubts and fears were common to her state,
Being with child; but when her child was born,
Then her new child was as herself renew'd,
Then the new mother came about her heart,
Then her good Philip was her all-in-all,
And that mysterious instinct wholly died.

   And where was Enoch? Prosperously sail'd
The ship 'Good Fortune,' tho' at setting forth
The Biscay, roughly ridging eastward, shook
And almost overwhelm'd her, yet unvext
She slipt across the summer of the world,
Then after a long tumble about the Cape
And frequent interchange of foul and fair,
She passing thro' the summer world again,
The breath of heaven came continually
And sent her sweetly by the golden isles,
Till silent in her oriental haven.

   There Enoch traded for himself, and bought
Quaint monsters for the market of those times,
A gilded dragon also for the babes.

   Less lucky her home-voyage: at first indeed
Thro' many a fair sea-circle, day by day,
Scarce-rocking, her full-busted figure-head

Stared o'er the ripple feathering from her bows:
Then follow'd calms, and then winds variable,
Then baffling, a long course of them; and last
Storm, such as drove her under moonless heavens
Till hard upon the cry of 'breakers' came
The crash of ruin, and the loss of all
But Enoch and two others. Half the night,
Buoy'd upon floating tackle and broken spars,
These drifted, stranding on an isle at morn
Rich, but the loneliest in a lonely sea.

   No want was there of human sustenance,
Soft fruitage, mighty nuts, and nourishing roots;
Nor save for pity was it hard to take
The helpless life so wild that it was tame.
There in a seaward-gazing mountain-gorge
They built, and thatch'd with leaves of palm, a hut,
Half hut, half native cavern. So the three,
Set in this Eden of all plenteousness,
Dwelt with eternal summer, ill-content.
For one, the youngest, hardly more than boy,
Hurt in that night of sudden ruin and wreck,
Lay lingering out a five-years' death-in-life.
They could not leave him. After he was gone,
The two remaining found a fallen stem;
And Enoch's comrade, careless of himself,
Fire-hollowing this in Indian fashion, fell
Sun-stricken, and that other lived alone.
In those two deaths he read God's warning 'wait.'

   The mountain wooded to the peak, the lawns
And winding glades high up like ways to heaven,
The slender coco's drooping crown of plumes,
The lightning flash of insect and of bird,
The lustre of the long convolvuluses
That coil'd around the stately stems, and ran
Even to the limit of the land, the glows
And glories of the broad belt of the world,—
All these he saw; but what he fain had seen
He could not see, the kindly human face,
Nor ever hear a kindly voice, but heard
The myriad shriek of wheeling ocean-fowl,
The league-long roller thundering on the reef,
The moving whisper of huge trees that branch'd

And blossom'd in the zenith, or the sweep
Of some precipitous rivulet to the wave,
As down the shore he ranged, or all day long
Sat often in the seaward-gazing gorge,
A shipwreck'd sailor, waiting for a sail.
No sail from day to day, but every day
The sunrise broken into scarlet shafts
Among the palms and ferns and precipices;
The blaze upon the waters to the east;
The blaze upon his island overhead;
The blaze upon the waters to the west;
Then the great stars that globed themselves in heaven,
The hollower-bellowing ocean, and again
The scarlet shafts of sunrise—but no sail.

   There often as he watch'd or seem'd to watch,
So still the golden lizard on him paused,
A phantom made of many phantoms moved
Before him haunting him, or he himself
Moved haunting people, things, and places, known
Far in a darker isle beyond the line;
The babes, their babble, Annie, the small house,
The climbing street, the mill, the leafy lanes,
The peacock yew-tree and the lonely Hall,
The horse he drove, the boat he sold, the chill
November dawns and dewy-glooming downs,
The gentle shower, the smell of dying leaves,
And the low moan of leaden-color'd seas.

   Once likewise, in the ringing of his ears,
Tho' faintly, merrily—far and far away—
He heard the pealing of his parish bells;
Then, tho' he knew not wherefore, started up
Shuddering, and when the beauteous hateful isle
Return'd upon him, had not his poor heart
Spoken with That which being everywhere
Lets none who speaks with Him seem all alone,
Surely the man had died of solitude.

   Thus over Enoch's early-silvering head
The sunny and rainy seasons came and went
Year after year. His hopes to see his own,
And pace the sacred old familiar fields,
Not yet had perish'd, when his lonely doom

Came suddenly to an end. Another ship—
She wanted water—blown by baffling winds,
Like the 'Good Fortune,' from her destined course,
Stay'd by this isle, not knowing where she lay;
For since the mate had seen at early dawn
Across a break on the mist-wreathen isle
The silent water slipping from the hills,
They sent a crew that landing burst away
In search of stream or fount, and fill'd the shores
With clamor. Downward from his mountain gorge
Stept the long-hair'd, long-bearded solitary,
Brown, looking hardly human, strangely clad,
Muttering and mumbling, idiot-like it seem'd,
With inarticulate rage, and making signs
They knew not what; and yet he led the way
To where the rivulets of sweet water ran,
And ever as he mingled with the crew,
And heard them talking, his long-bounden tongue
Was loosen'd, till he made them understand;
Whom, when their casks were fill'd, they took aboard.
And there the tale he utter'd brokenly,
Scarce-credited at first but more and more,
Amazed and melted all who listen'd to it;
And clothes they gave him and free passage home,
But oft he work'd among the rest and shook
His isolation from him. None of these
Came from his country, or could answer him,
If question'd, aught of what he cared to know.
And dull the voyage was with long delays,
The vessel scarce sea-worthy; but evermore
His fancy fled before the lazy wind
Returning, till beneath a clouded moon
He like a lover down thro' all his blood
Drew in the dewy meadowy morning-breath
Of England, blown across her ghostly wall.
And that same morning officers and men
Levied a kindly tax upon themselves,
Pitying the lonely man, and gave him it;
Then moving up the coast they landed him,
Even in that harbor whence he sail'd before.

   There Enoch spoke no word to any one,
But homeward—home—what home? had he a home?—

His home, he walk'd. Bright was that afternoon,
Sunny but chill; till drawn thro' either chasm,
Where either haven open'd on the deeps,
Roll'd a sea-haze and whelm'd the world in gray,
Cut off the length of highway on before,
And left but narrow breadth to left and right
Of wither'd holt or tilth or pasturage.
On the nigh-naked tree the robin piped
Disconsolate, and thro' the dripping haze
The dead weight of the dead leaf bore it down.
Thicker the drizzle grew, deeper the gloom;
Last, as it seem'd, a great mist-blotted light
Flared on him, and he came upon the place.

Then down the long street having slowly stolen,
His heart foreshadowing all calamity,
His eyes upon the stones, he reach'd the home
Where Annie lived and loved him, and his babes
In those far-off seven happy years were born;
But finding neither light nor murmur there—
A bill of sale gleam'd thro' the drizzle—crept
Still downward thinking, 'dead or dead to me!'

Down to the pool and narrow wharf he went,
Seeking a tavern which of old he knew,
A front of timber-crost antiquity,
So propt, worm-eaten, ruinously old,
He thought it must have gone; but he was gone
Who kept it, and his widow Miriam Lane,
With daily-dwindling profits held the house;
A haunt of brawling seamen once, but now
Stiller, with yet a bed for wandering men.
There Enoch rested silent many days.

But Miriam Lane was good and garrulous,
Nor let him be, but often breaking in,
Told him, with other annals of the port,
Not knowing—Enoch was so brown, so bow'd,
So broken—all the story of his house:
His baby's death, her growing poverty,
How Philip put her little ones to school,
And kept them in it, his long wooing her,
Her slow consent and marriage, and the birth
Of Philip's child; and o'er his countenance

No shadow past, nor motion. Any one,
Regarding, well had deem'd he felt the tale
Less than the teller; only when she closed,
'Enoch, poor man, was cast away and lost,'
He, shaking his gray head pathetically,
Repeated muttering, 'cast away and lost;'
Again in deeper inward whispers, 'lost!'

But Enoch yearn'd to see her face again:
'If I might look on her sweet face again,
And know that she is happy.' So the thought
Haunted and harass'd him, and drove him forth,
At evening when the dull November day
Was growing duller twilight, to the hill.
There he sat down gazing on all below;
There did a thousand memories roll upon him,
Unspeakable for sadness. By and by
The ruddy square of comfortable light,
Far-blazing from the rear of Philip's house,
Allured him, as the beacon-blaze allures
The bird of passage, till he madly strikes
Against it and beats out his weary life.

For Philip's dwelling fronted on the street,
The latest house to landward; but behind,
With one small gate that open'd on the waste,
Flourish'd a little garden square and wall'd,
And in it throve an ancient evergreen,
A yew-tree, and all round it ran a walk
Of shingle, and a walk divided it.
But Enoch shunn'd the middle walk and stole
Up by the wall, behind the yew; and thence
That which he better might have shunn'd, if griefs
Like his have worse or better, Enoch saw.

For cups and silver on the burnish'd board
Sparkled and shone; so genial was the hearth;
And on the right hand of the hearth he saw
Philip, the slighted suitor of old times,
Stout, rosy, with his babe across his knees;
And o'er her second father stoopt a girl,
A later but a loftier Annie Lee,
Fair-hair'd and tall, and from her lifted hand
Dangled a length of ribbon and a ring

To tempt the babe, who rear'd his creasy arms,
Caught at and ever miss'd it, and they laugh'd;
And on the left hand of the hearth he saw
The mother glancing often toward her babe,
But turning now and then to speak with him,
Her son, who stood beside her tall and strong,
And saying that which pleased him, for he smiled.

Now when the dead man come to life beheld
His wife his wife no more, and saw the babe
Hers, yet not his, upon the father's knee,
And all the warmth, the peace, the happiness,
And his own children tall and beautiful,
And him, that other, reigning in his place,
Lord of his rights and of his children's love—
Then he, tho' Miriam Lane had told him all,
Because things seen are mightier than things heard,
Stagger'd and shook, holding the branch, and fear'd
To send abroad a shrill and terrible cry,
Which in one moment, like the blast of doom,
Would shatter all the happiness of the hearth.

He therefore turning softly like a thief,
Lest the harsh shingle should grate underfoot,
And feeling all along the garden-wall,
Lest he should swoon and tumble and be found,
Crept to the gate, and open'd it and closed,
As lightly as a sick man's chamber-door,
Behind him, and came out upon the waste.

And there he would have knelt, but that his knees
Were feeble, so that falling prone he dug
His fingers into the wet earth, and pray'd:

'Too hard to bear! why did they take me thence?
O God Almighty, blessed Saviour, Thou
That didst uphold me on my lonely isle,
Uphold me, Father, in my loneliness
A little longer! aid me, give me strength
Not to tell her, never to let her know.
Help me not to break in upon her peace.
My children too! must I not speak to these?
They know me not. I should betray myself.
Never! no father's kiss for me—the girl

So like her mother, and the boy, my son.'

There speech and thought and nature fail'd a little,
And he lay tranced; but when he rose and paced
Back toward his solitary home again,
All down the long and narrow street he went
Beating it in upon his weary brain,
As tho' it were the burthen of a song,
'Not to tell her, never to let her know.'

He was not all unhappy. His resolve
Upbore him, and firm faith, and evermore
Prayer from a living source within the will,
And beating up thro' all the bitter world,
Like fountains of sweet water in the sea,
Kept him a living soul. 'This miller's wife,'
He said to Miriam, 'that you spoke about,
Has she no fear that her first husband lives?'
'Ay, ay, poor soul,' said Miriam, 'fear enow!
If you could tell her you had seen him dead,
Why, that would be her comfort;' and he thought,
'After the Lord has call'd me she shall know,
I wait His time;' and Enoch set himself,
Scorning an alms, to work whereby to live.
Almost to all things could he turn his hand.
Cooper he was and carpenter, and wrought
To make the boatmen fishing-nets, or help'd
At lading and unlading the tall barks
That brought the stinted commerce of those days,
Thus earn'd a scanty living for himself.
Yet since he did but labor for himself,
Work without hope, there was not life in it
Whereby the man could live; and as the year
Roll'd itself round again to meet the day
When Enoch had return'd, a languor came
Upon him, gentle sickness, gradually
Weakening the man, till he could do no more,
But kept the house, his chair, and last his bed.
And Enoch bore his weakness cheerfully.
For sure no gladlier does the stranded wreck
See thro' the gray skirts of a lifting squall
The boat that bears the hope of life approach
To save the life despair'd of, than he saw

Death dawning on him, and the close of all.

   For thro' that dawning gleam'd a kindlier hope
On Enoch thinking, 'after I am gone,
Then may she learn I loved her to the last.'
He call'd aloud for Miriam Lane and said:
'Woman, I have a secret—only swear,
Before I tell you—swear upon the book
Not to reveal it, till you see me dead.'
'Dead,' clamor'd the good woman, 'hear him talk!
I warrant, man, that we shall bring you round.'
'Swear,' added Enoch sternly, 'on the book;'
And on the book, half-frighted, Miriam swore.
Then Enoch rolling his gray eyes upon her,
'Did you know Enoch Arden of this town?'
'Know him?' she said, 'I knew him far away.
Ay, ay, I mind him coming down the street;
Held his head high, and cared for no man, he.'
Slowly and sadly Enoch answer'd her:
'His head is low, and no man cares for him.
I think I have not three days more to live;
I am the man.' At which the woman gave
A half-incredulous, half-hysterical cry:
'You Arden, you! nay,—sure he was a foot
Higher than you be.' Enoch said again:
'My God has bow'd me down to what I am;
My grief and solitude have broken me;
Nevertheless, know you that I am he
Who married—but that name has twice been changed—
I married her who married Philip Ray.
Sit, listen.' Then he told her of his voyage,
His wreck, his lonely life, his coming back,
His gazing in on Annie, his resolve,
And how he kept it. As the woman heard,
Fast flow'd the current of her easy tears,
While in her heart she yearn'd incessantly
To rush abroad all round the little haven,
Proclaiming Enoch Arden and his woes;
But awed and promise-bounden she forbore,
Saying only, 'See your bairns before you go!
Eh, let me fetch 'em, Arden,' and arose
Eager to bring them down, for Enoch hung
A moment on her words, but then replied:

'Woman, disturb me not now at the last,
But let me hold my purpose till I die.
Sit down again; mark me and understand,
While I have power to speak. I charge you now,
When you shall see her, tell her that I died
Blessing her, praying for her, loving her;
Save for the bar between us, loving her
As when she laid her head beside my own.
And tell my daughter Annie, whom I saw
So like her mother, that my latest breath
Was spent in blessing her and praying for her.
And tell my son that I died blessing him.
And say to Philip that I blest him too;
He never meant us anything but good.
But if my children care to see me dead,
Who hardly knew me living, let them come,
I am their father; but she must not come,
For my dead face would vex her after-life.
And now there is but one of all my blood
Who will embrace me in the world-to-be.
This hair is his, she cut it off and gave it,
And I have borne it with me all these years,
And thought to bear it with me to my grave;
But now my mind is changed, for I shall see him,
My babe in bliss. Wherefore when I am gone,
Take, give her this, for it may comfort her;
It will moreover be a token to her
That I am he.'

      He ceased; and Miriam Lane
Made such a voluble answer promising all,
That once again he roll'd his eyes upon her
Repeating all he wish'd, and once again
She promised.

      Then the third night after this,
While Enoch slumber'd motionless and pale,
And Miriam watch'd and dozed at intervals,
There came so loud a calling of the sea
That all the houses in the haven rang.
He woke, he rose, he spread his arms abroad,
Crying with a loud voice, 'A sail! a sail!
I am saved;' and so fell back and spoke no more.

So past the strong heroic soul away.
And when they buried him the little port
Had seldom seen a costlier funeral.

❧

FLOWER in the crannied wall,
I pluck you out of the crannies,
I hold you here, root and all, in my hand,
Little flower—but *if* I could understand
What you are, root and all, and all in all,
I should know what God and man is.

Rizpah
17—

I

WAILING, wailing, wailing, the wind over land and sea—
And Willy's voice in the wind, 'O mother, come out to me !'
Why should he call me to-night, when he knows that I cannot go ?
For the downs are as bright as day, and the full moon stares at the snow.

II

We should be seen, my dear; they would spy us out of the town.
The loud black nights for us, and the storm rushing over the down,
When I cannot see my own hand, but am led by the creak of the
    chain,
And grovel and grope for my son till I find myself drenched with the
    rain.

III

Anything fallen again ? nay—what was there left to fall ?
I have taken them home, I have number'd the bones, I have hidden
    them all.
What am I saying ? and what are *you?* do you come as a spy ?
Falls ? what falls ? who knows ? As the tree falls so must it lie.

IV

Who let her in ? how long has she been ? you—what have you heard ?
Why did you sit so quiet ? you never have spoken a word.
O—to pray with me—yes—a lady—none of their spies—
But the night has crept into my heart, and begun to darken my eyes.

V

Ah—you, that have lived so soft, what should *you* know of the night,
The blast and the burning shame and the bitter frost and the fright ?
I have done it, while you were asleep—you were only made for the day.
I have gather'd my baby together—and now you may go your way.

VI

Nay—for it's kind of you, madam, to sit by an old dying wife.
But say nothing hard of my boy, I have only an hour of life.
I kiss'd my boy in the prison, before he went out to die.
'They dared me to do it,' he said, and he never has told me a lie.
I whipt him for robbing an orchard once when he was but a child—
'The farmer dared me to do it,' he said; he was always so wild—
And idle—and could n't be idle—my Willy—he never could rest.
The King should have made him a soldier, he would have been one of
    his best.

VII

But he lived with a lot of wild mates, and they never would let him be
    good;
They swore that he dare not rob the mail, and he swore that he would;
And he took no life, but he took one purse, and when all was done
He flung it among his fellows—'I'll none of it,' said my son.

VIII

I came into court to the judge and the lawyers. I told them my tale,
God's own truth—but they kill'd him, they kill'd him for robbing the
    mail.
They hang'd him in chains for a show—we had always borne a good
    name—
To be hang'd for a thief—and then put away—is n't that enough
    shame ?

Dust to dust—low down—let us hide ! but they set him so high
That all the ships of the world could stare at him, passing by.
God 'ill pardon the hell-black raven and horrible fowls of the air,
But not the black heart of the lawyer who kill'd him and hang'd him there.

IX

And the jailer forced me away. I had bid him my last good-bye;
They had fasten'd the door of his cell. 'O mother !' I heard him cry.
I could n't get back tho' I tried, he had something further to say,
And now I never shall know it. The jailer forced me away.

X

Then since I could n't but hear that cry of my boy that was dead,
They seized me and shut me up: they fasten'd me down on my bed.
'Mother, O mother !'—he call'd in the dark to me year after year—
They beat me for that, they beat me—you know that I could n't but hear;
And then at the last they found I had grown so stupid and still.
They let me abroad again—but the creatures had worked their will.

XI

Flesh of my flesh was gone, but bone of my bone was left—
I stole them all from the lawyers—and you, will you call it a theft ?—
My baby, the bones that had suck'd me, the bones that had laughed and had cried—
Theirs ? O, no ! they are mine—not theirs—they had moved in my side.

XII

Do you think I was scared by the bones ? I kiss'd 'em, I buried 'em all—
I can't dig deep, I am old—in the night by the churchyard wall.
My Willy 'ill rise up whole when the trumpet of judgment 'ill sound,
But I charge you never to say that I laid him in holy ground.

XIII

They would scratch him up—they would hang him again on the cursed tree.
Sin ? O, yes, we are sinners, I know—let all that be,

And read me a Bible verse of the Lord's goodwill toward men—
'Full of compassion and mercy, the Lord'—let me hear it again;
'Full of compassion and mercy—long-suffering.' Yes, O, yes!
For the lawyer is born but to murder—the Saviour lives but to bless.
He'll never put on the black cap except for the worst of the worst,
And the first may be last—I have heard it in church—and the last may be first.
Suffering—O, long-suffering—yes, as the Lord must know,
Year after year in the mist and the wind and the shower and the snow.

XIV

Heard, have you? what? they have told you he never repented his sin.
How do they know it? are *they* his mother? are *you* of his kin?
Heard! have you ever heard, when the storm on the downs began,
The wind that 'ill wail like a child and the sea that 'ill moan like a man?

XV

Election, Election, and Reprobation—it's all very well.
But I go to-night to my boy, and I shall not find him in hell.
For I cared so much for my boy that the Lord has look'd into my care,
And He means me I'm sure to be happy with Willy, I know not where.

XVI

And if *he* be lost—but to save *my* soul, that is all your desire—
Do you think that I care for *my* soul if my boy be gone to the fire?
I have been with God in the dark—go, go, you may leave me alone—
You never have borne a child—you are just as hard as a stone.

XVII

Madam, I beg your pardon! I think that you mean to be kind,
But I cannot hear what you say for my Willy's voice in the wind—
The snow and the sky so bright—he used but to call in the dark,
And he calls to me now from the church and not from the gibbet—for hark!
Nay—you can hear it yourself—it is coming—shaking the walls—
Willy—the moon's in a cloud—Good-night. I am going. He calls.

The Revenge

A BALLAD OF THE FLEET

I

At Flores in the Azores Sir Richard Grenville lay,
And a pinnace, like a flutter'd bird, came flying from far away:
'Spanish ships of war at sea! we have sighted fifty-three!'
Then sware Lord Thomas Howard: ' 'Fore God I am no coward;
But I cannot meet them here, for my ships are out of gear,
And the half my men are sick. I must fly, but follow quick.
We are six ships of the line; can we fight with fifty-three?'

II

Then spake Sir Richard Grenville: 'I know you are no coward;
You fly them for a moment to fight with them again.
But I've ninety men and more that are lying sick ashore.
I should count myself the coward if I left them, my Lord Howard,
To these Inquisition dogs and the devildoms of Spain.'

III

So Lord Howard past away with five ships of war that day,
Till he melted like a cloud in the silent summer heaven;
But Sir Richard bore in hand all his sick men from the land
Very carefully and slow,
Men of Bideford in Devon,
And we laid them on the ballast down below;
For we brought them all aboard,
And they blest him in their pain, that they were not left to Spain,
To the thumb-screw and the stake, for the glory of the Lord.

IV

He had only a hundred seamen to work the ship and to fight,
And he sailed away from Flores till the Spaniard came in sight,
With his huge sea-castles heaving upon the weather bow.
'Shall we fight or shall we fly?
Good Sir Richard, tell us now,
For to fight is but to die!
There'll be little of us left by the time this sun be set.'

And Sir Richard said again: 'We be all good English men.
Let us bang these dogs of Seville, the children of the devil,
For I never turn'd my back upon Don or devil yet.'

V

Sir Richard spoke and he laugh'd, and we roar'd a hurrah, and so
The little Revenge ran on sheer into the heart of the foe,
With her hundred fighters on deck, and her ninety sick below;
For half of their fleet to the right and half to the left were seen,
And the little Revenge ran on thro' the long sea-lane between.

VI

Thousands of their soldiers look'd down from their decks and laugh'd,
Thousands of their seamen made mock at the mad little craft
Running on and on, till delay'd
By their mountain-like San Philip that, of fifteen hundred tons,
And up-shadowing high above us with her yawning tiers of guns,
Took the breath from our sails, and we stay'd.

VII

And while now the great San Philip hung above us like a cloud
Whence the thunderbolt will fall
Long and loud,
Four galleons drew away
From the Spanish fleet that day,
And two upon the larboard and two upon the starboard lay,
And the battle-thunder broke from them all.

VIII

But anon the great San Philip, she bethought herself and went,
Having that within her womb that had left her ill content;
And the rest they came aboard us, and they fought us hand to hand,
For a dozen times they came with their pikes and musqueteers,
And a dozen times we shook 'em off as a dog that shakes his ears
When he leaps from the water to the land.

IX

And the sun went down, and the stars came out far over the summer
    sea,

But never a moment ceased the fight of the one and the fifty-three.
Ship after ship, the whole night long, their high-built galleons came,
Ship after ship, the whole night long, with her battle-thunder and flame;
Ship after ship, the whole night long, drew back with her dead and her shame.
For some were sunk and many were shatter'd, and so could fight us no more—
God of battles, was ever a battle like this in the world before ?

X

For he said, 'Fight on ! Fight on !'
Tho' his vessel was all but a wreck;
And it chanced that, when half of the short summer night was gone,
With a grisly wound to be drest he had left the deck,
But a bullet struck him that was dressing it suddenly dead,
And himself he was wounded again in the side and the head,
And he said, 'Fight on ! fight on !'

XI

And the night went down, and the sun smiled out far over the summer sea,
And the Spanish fleet with broken sides lay round us all in a ring;
But they dared not touch us again, for they fear'd that we still could sting,
So they watch'd what the end would be.
And we had not fought them in vain,
But in perilous plight were we,
Seeing forty of our poor hundred were slain,
And half of the rest of us maim'd for life
In the crash of the cannonades and the desperate strife;
And the sick men down in the hold were most of them stark and cold,
And the pikes were all broken or bent, and the powder was all of it spent;
And the masts and the rigging were lying over the side;
But Sir Richard cried in his English pride:
'We have fought such a fight for a day and a night
As may never be fought again !
We have won great glory, my men !
And a day less or more
At sea or ashore,

We die—does it matter when?
Sink me the ship, Master Gunner—sink her, split her in twain!
Fall into the hands of God, not into the hands of Spain!'

XII

And the gunner said, 'Ay, ay,' but the seamen made reply:
'We have children, we have wives,
And the Lord hath spared our lives.
We will make the Spaniard promise, if we yield, to let us go;
We shall live to fight again and to strike another blow.'
And the lion there lay dying, and they yielded to the foe.

XIII

And the stately Spanish men to their flagship bore him then,
Where they laid him by the mast, old Sir Richard caught at last,
And they praised him to his face with their courtly foreign grace;
But he rose upon their decks, and he cried:
'I have fought for Queen and Faith like a valiant man and true;
I have only done my duty as a man is bound to do.
With a joyful spirit I Sir Richard Grenville die!'
And he fell upon their decks, and he died.

XIV

And they stared at the dead that had been so valiant and true,
And had holden the power and glory of Spain so cheap
That he dared her with one little ship and his English few;
Was he devil or man? He was devil for aught they knew,
But they sank his body with honor down into the deep,
And they mann'd the Revenge with a swarthier alien crew,
And away she sail'd with her loss and long'd for her own;
When a wind from the lands they had ruin'd awoke from sleep,
And the water began to heave and the weather to moan,
And or ever that evening ended a great gale blew,
And a wave like the wave that is raised by an earthquake grew,
Till it smote on their hulls and their sails and their masts and their flags,
And the whole sea plunged and fell on the shot-shatter'd navy of Spain,
And the little Revenge herself went down by the island crags
To be lost evermore in the main.

To Virgil

**WRITTEN AT THE REQUEST OF THE MANTUANS
FOR THE NINETEENTH CENTENARY OF
VIRGIL'S DEATH**

I

Roman Virgil, thou that singest
    Ilion's lofty temples robed in fire,
Ilion falling, Rome arising,
    wars, and filial faith, and Dido's pyre;

II

Landscape-lover, lord of language
    more than he that sang the 'Works and Days,'
All the chosen coin of fancy
    flashing out from many a golden phrase;

III

Thou that singest wheat and woodland,
    tilth and vineyard, hive and horse and herd;
All the charm of all the Muses
    often flowering in a lonely word;

IV

Poet of the happy Tityrus
    piping underneath his beechen bowers;
Poet of the poet-satyr
    whom the laughing shepherd bound with flowers;

V

Chanter of the Pollio, glorying
    in the blissful years again to be.
Summers of the snakeless meadow,
    unlaborious earth and oarless sea;

VI

Thou that seest Universal
    Nature moved by Universal Mind;

Thou majestic in thy sadness
    at the doubtful doom of human kind;

VII

Light among the vanish'd ages;
    star that gildest yet this phantom shore;
Golden branch amid the shadows,
    kings and realms that pass to rise no more;

VIII

Now thy Forum roars no longer,
    fallen every purple Cæsar's dome—
Tho' thine ocean-roll of rhythm
    sound forever of Imperial Rome—

IX

Now the Rome of slaves hath perish'd,
    and the Rome of freemen holds her place,
I, from out the Northern Island
    sunder'd once from all the human race,

X

I salute thee, Mantovano,
    I that loved thee since my day began,
Wielder of the stateliest measure
    ever moulded by the lips of man.

Merlin and the Gleam

I

    O YOUNG Mariner,
    You from the haven
    Under the sea-cliff,
    You that are watching
    The gray Magician
    With eyes of wonder,
    I am Merlin,
    And *I* am dying,
    I am Merlin
    Who follow the Gleam.

II

Mighty the Wizard
Who found me at sunrise
Sleeping, and woke me
And learn'd me Magic !
Great the Master,
And sweet the Magic,
When over the valley,
In early summers,
Over the mountain,
On human faces,
And all around me,
Moving to melody,
Floated the Gleam.

III

Once at the croak of a Raven who crost it
A barbarous people,
Blind to the magic
And deaf to the melody,
Snarl'd at and cursed me.
A demon vext me,
The light retreated,
The landskip darken'd,
The melody deaden'd,
The Master whisper'd,
'Follow the Gleam.'

IV

Then to the melody,
Over a wilderness
Gliding, and glancing at
Elf of the woodland,
Gnome of the cavern,
Griffin and Giant,
And dancing of Fairies
In desolate hollows,
And wraiths of the mountain,
And rolling of dragons
By warble of water,

Or cataract music
Of falling torrents,
Flitted the Gleam.

V

Down from the mountain
And over the level,
And streaming and shining on
Silent river,
Silvery willow,
Pasture and plowland,
Innocent maidens,
Garrulous children,
Homestead and harvest,
Reaper and gleaner,
And rough-ruddy faces
Of lowly labor,
Slided the Gleam—

VI

Then, with a melody
Stronger and statelier,
Led me at length
To the city and palace
Of Arthur the King;
Touch'd at the golden
Cross of the churches,
Flash'd on the tournament,
Flicker'd and bicker'd
From helmet to helmet,
And last on the forehead
Of Arthur the blameless
Rested the Gleam.

VII

Clouds and darkness
Closed upon Camelot;
Arthur had vanish'd
I knew not whither,
The king who loved me,
And cannot die;

For out of the darkness
Silent and slowly
The Gleam, that had waned to a wintry glimmer
On icy fallow
And faded forest,
Drew to the valley
Named of the shadow,
And slowly brightening
Out of the glimmer,
And slowly moving again to a melody
Yearningly tender,
Fell on the shadow,
No longer a shadow,
But clothed with the Gleam.

VIII

And broader and brighter
The Gleam flying onward,
Wed to the melody,
Sang thro' the world;
And slower and fainter,
Old and weary,
But eager to follow,
I saw, whenever
In passing it glanced upon
Hamlet or city,
That under the Crosses
The dead man's garden,
The mortal hillock,
Would break into blossom;
And so to the land's
Last limit I came—
And can no longer,
But die rejoicing,
For thro' the Magic
Of Him the Mighty,
Who taught me in childhood,
There on the border
Of boundless Ocean,
And all but in Heaven
Hovers the Gleam.

IX

Not of the sunlight,
Not of the moonlight,
Not of the starlight!
O young Mariner,
Down to the haven,
Call your companions,
Launch your vessel
And crowd your canvas,
And, ere it vanishes
Over the margin,
After it, follow it,
Follow the Gleam.

Crossing the Bar

SUNSET and evening star,
   And one clear call for me!
And may there be no moaning of the bar,
   When I put out to sea,

But such a tide as moving seems asleep,
   Too full for sound and foam,
When that which drew from out the boundless deep
   Turns again home.

Twilight and evening bell,
   And after that the dark!
And may there be no sadness of farewell,
   When I embark;

For tho' from out our bourne of Time and Place
   The flood may bear me far,
I hope to see my Pilot face to face
   When I have crost the bar.

Alphabetical List of Titles

	page
Beggar Maid, The	36
"Break, break, break"	36
Brook, The (excerpts)	43
Charge of the Light Brigade, The	52
"Come down, O maid"	40
"Come into the garden, Maud"	41
Crossing the Bar	89
Enoch Arden	53
"Flower in the crannied wall"	56
"Home they brought her warrior dead"	39
Lady Clara Vere de Vere	14
Lady of Shalott, The	3
Locksley Hall	29
Lotos-Eaters, The	20
Mariana	1
Maud (excerpt)	41
May Queen, The	16
Merlin and the Gleam	85
"Now sleeps the crimson petal"	39
Ode on the Death of the Duke of Wellington	44

Œnone	7
"O Swallow, Swallow"	38
Princess, The (excerpts)	37ff.
Revenge, The	80
Rizpah	76
Saint Agnes' Eve	35
Song of the Brook, The	43
"Splendor falls, The"	37
"Sweet and Low"	37
"Tears, idle tears"	38
Tithonus	27
To Virgil	84
Ulysses	25

Alphabetical List of First Lines

page

At Flores in the Azores Sir Richard Grenville lay	80
Break, break, break	36
Bury the Great Duke	44
Come down, O maid, from yonder mountain height	40
Come into the garden, Maud	41
Comrades, leave me here a little, while as yet 't is early morn	29
'Courage!' he said, and pointed toward the land	20
Deep on the convent-roof the snows	35
Flower in the crannied wall	76
Half a league, half a league	52
Her arms across her breast she laid	36
Home they brought her warrior dead	39
I come from haunts of coot and hern	43
It little profits that an idle king	25
Lady Clara Vere de Vere	14
Long lines of cliff breaking have left a chasm	53
Now sleeps the crimson petal, now the white	39
On either side the river lie	3
O Swallow, Swallow, flying, flying south	38

O young Mariner	85
Roman Virgil, thou that singest	84
Sunset and evening star	89
Sweet and low, sweet and low	37
Tears, idle tears, I know not what they mean	38
There lies a vale in Ida, lovelier	7
The splendor falls on castle walls	37
The woods decay, the woods decay and fall	27
Wailing, wailing, wailing, the wind over land and sea—	76
With blackest moss the flower-plots	1
You must wake and call me early, call me early, mother dear	16

DOVER·THRIFT·EDITIONS

All books complete and unabridged. All 5³⁄₁₆″ × 8¼″, paperbound.
Just $1.00–$2.00 in U.S.A.

POETRY

Dover Beach and Other Poems, Matthew Arnold. 112pp. 28037-3 $1.00

Bhagavadgita, Bhagavadgita. 112pp. 27782-8 $1.00

Songs of Innocence and Songs of Experience, William Blake. 64pp. 27051-3 $1.00

Sonnets from the Portuguese and Other Poems, Elizabeth Barrett Browning. 64pp. 27052-1 $1.00

My Last Duchess and Other Poems, Robert Browning. 128pp. 27783-6 $1.00

Poems and Songs, Robert Burns. 96pp. 26863-2 $1.00

Selected Poems, George Gordon, Lord Byron. 112pp. 27784-4 $1.00

The Rime of the Ancient Mariner and Other Poems, Samuel Taylor Coleridge. 80pp. 27266-4 $1.00

Selected Poems, Emily Dickinson. 64pp. 26466-1 $1.00

Selected Poems, John Donne. 96pp. 27788-7 $1.00

The Rubáiyát of Omar Khayyám: First and Fifth Editions, Edward FitzGerald. 64pp. 26467-X $1.00

A Boy's Will and North of Boston, Robert Frost. 112pp. (Available in U.S. only.) 26866-7 $1.00

The Road Not Taken and Other Poems, Robert Frost. 64pp. (Available in U.S. only) 27550-7 $1.00

A Shropshire Lad, A. E. Housman. 64pp. 26468-8 $1.00

Lyric Poems, John Keats. 80pp. 26871-3 $1.00

The Book of Psalms, King James Bible. 128pp. 27541-8 $1.00

Gunga Din and Other Favorite Poems, Rudyard Kipling. 80pp. 26471-8 $1.00

The Congo and Other Poems, Vachel Lindsay. 96pp. 27272-9 $1.00

Favorite Poems, Henry Wadsworth Longfellow. 96pp. 27273-7 $1.00

Spoon River Anthology, Edgar Lee Masters. 144pp. 27275-3 $1.00

Renascence and Other Poems, Edna St. Vincent Millay. 64pp. (Available in U.S. only.) 26873-X $1.00

Selected Poems, John Milton. 128pp. 27554-X $1.00

Great Sonnets, Paul Negri (ed.). 96pp. 28052-7 $1.00

The Raven and Other Favorite Poems, Edgar Allan Poe. 64pp. 26685-0 $1.00

Essay on Man and Other Poems, Alexander Pope. 128pp. 28053-5 $1.00

Goblin Market and Other Poems, Christina Rossetti. 64pp. 28055-1 $1.00

Chicago Poems, Carl Sandburg. 80pp. 28057-8 $1.00

The Shooting of Dan McGrew and Other Poems, Robert Service. 96pp. 27556-6 $1.00

Complete Songs from the Plays, William Shakespeare. 80pp. 27801-8 $1.00

Complete Sonnets, William Shakespeare. 80pp. 26686-9 $1.00

Selected Poems, Percy Bysshe Shelley. 128pp. 27558-2 $1.00

Selected Poems, Alfred Lord Tennyson. 112pp. 27282-6 $1.00

Christmas Carols: Complete Verses, Shane Weller (ed.). 64pp. 27397-0 $1.00

DOVER · THRIFT · EDITIONS

All books complete and unabridged. All 5³⁄₁₆″ × 8¼″, paperbound.
Just $1.00–$2.00 in U.S.A.

POETRY

GREAT LOVE POEMS, Shane Weller (ed.). 128pp. 27284-2 $1.00
SELECTED POEMS, Walt Whitman. 128pp. 26878-0 $1.00
THE BALLAD OF READING GAOL AND OTHER POEMS, Oscar Wilde. 64pp. 27072-6 $1.00
FAVORITE POEMS, William Wordsworth. 80pp. 27073-4 $1.00
EARLY POEMS, William Butler Yeats. 128pp. 27808-5 $1.00

FICTION

FLATLAND: A ROMANCE OF MANY DIMENSIONS, Edwin A. Abbott. 96pp. 27263-X $1.00
BEOWULF, Beowulf (trans. by R. K. Gordon). 64pp. 27264-8 $1.00
CIVIL WAR STORIES, Ambrose Bierce. 128pp. 28038-1 $1.00
ALICE'S ADVENTURES IN WONDERLAND, Lewis Carroll. 96pp. 27543-4 $1.00
O PIONEERS!, Willa Cather. 128pp. 27785-2 $1.00
FIVE GREAT SHORT STORIES, Anton Chekhov. 96pp. 26463-7 $1.00
FAVORITE FATHER BROWN STORIES, G. K. Chesterton. 96pp. 27545-0 $1.00
THE AWAKENING, Kate Chopin. 128pp. 27786-0 $1.00
HEART OF DARKNESS, Joseph Conrad. 80pp. 26464-5 $1.00
THE SECRET SHARER AND OTHER STORIES, Joseph Conrad. 128pp. 27546-9 $1.00
THE OPEN BOAT AND OTHER STORIES, Stephen Crane. 128pp. 27547-7 $1.00
THE RED BADGE OF COURAGE, Stephen Crane. 112pp. 26465-3 $1.00
A CHRISTMAS CAROL, Charles Dickens. 80pp. 26865-9 $1.00
THE CRICKET ON THE HEARTH AND OTHER CHRISTMAS STORIES, Charles Dickens. 128pp. 28039-X $1.00
NOTES FROM THE UNDERGROUND, Fyodor Dostoyevsky. 96pp. 27053-X $1.00
SIX GREAT SHERLOCK HOLMES STORIES, Sir Arthur Conan Doyle. 112pp. 27055-6 $1.00
WHERE ANGELS FEAR TO TREAD, E. M. Forster. 128pp. (Available in U.S. only) 27791-7 $1.00
THE OVERCOAT AND OTHER SHORT STORIES, Nikolai Gogol. 112pp. 27057-2 $1.00
GREAT GHOST STORIES, John Grafton (ed.). 112pp. 27270-2 $1.00
THE LUCK OF ROARING CAMP AND OTHER SHORT STORIES, Bret Harte. 96pp. 27271-0 $1.00
THE SCARLET LETTER, Nathaniel Hawthorne. 192pp. 28048-9 $2.00
YOUNG GOODMAN BROWN AND OTHER SHORT STORIES, Nathaniel Hawthorne. 128pp. 27060-2 $1.00
THE GIFT OF THE MAGI AND OTHER SHORT STORIES, O. Henry. 96pp. 27061-0 $1.00
THE NUTCRACKER AND THE GOLDEN POT, E. T. A. Hoffmann. 128pp. 27806-9 $1.00
THE BEAST IN THE JUNGLE AND OTHER STORIES, Henry James. 128pp. 27552-3 $1.00
THE TURN OF THE SCREW, Henry James. 96pp. 26684-2 $1.00
DUBLINERS, James Joyce. 160pp. 26870-5 $1.00
A PORTRAIT OF THE ARTIST AS A YOUNG MAN, James Joyce. 192pp. 28050-0 $2.00

DOVER·THRIFT·EDITIONS

All books complete and unabridged. All 5³⁄₁₆" × 8¼", paperbound.
Just $1.00–$2.00 in U.S.A.

FICTION

THE MAN WHO WOULD BE KING AND OTHER STORIES, Rudyard Kipling. 128pp. 28051-9 $1.00
SELECTED SHORT STORIES, D. H. Lawrence. 128pp. 27794-1 $1.00
GREEN TEA AND OTHER GHOST STORIES, J. Sheridan LeFanu. 96pp. 27795-X $1.00
THE CALL OF THE WILD, Jack London. 64pp. 26472-6 $1.00
FIVE GREAT SHORT STORIES, Jack London. 96pp. 27063-7 $1.00
WHITE FANG, Jack London. 160pp. 26968-X $1.00
THE NECKLACE AND OTHER SHORT STORIES, Guy de Maupassant. 128pp. 27064-5 $1.00
BARTLEBY AND BENITO CERENO, Herman Melville. 112pp. 26473-4 $1.00
THE GOLD-BUG AND OTHER TALES, Edgar Allan Poe. 128pp. 26875-6 $1.00
THE QUEEN OF SPADES AND OTHER STORIES, Alexander Pushkin. 128pp. 28054-3 $1.00
THREE LIVES, Gertrude Stein. 176pp. 28059-4 $2.00
THE STRANGE CASE OF DR. JEKYLL AND MR. HYDE, Robert Louis Stevenson. 64pp. 26688-5 $1.00
TREASURE ISLAND, Robert Louis Stevenson. 160pp. 27559-0 $1.00
THE KREUTZER SONATA AND OTHER SHORT STORIES, Leo Tolstoy. 144pp. 27805-0 $1.00
ADVENTURES OF HUCKLEBERRY FINN, Mark Twain. 224pp. 28061-6 $2.00
THE MYSTERIOUS STRANGER AND OTHER STORIES, Mark Twain. 128pp. 27069-6 $1.00
CANDIDE, Voltaire (François-Marie Arouet). 112pp. 26689-3 $1.00
THE INVISIBLE MAN, H. G. Wells. 112pp. (Available in U.S. only.) 27071-8 $1.00
ETHAN FROME, Edith Wharton. 96pp. 26690-7 $1.00
THE PICTURE OF DORIAN GRAY, Oscar Wilde. 192pp. 27807-7 $1.00

NONFICTION

THE DEVIL'S DICTIONARY, Ambrose Bierce. 144pp. 27542-6 $1.00
THE SOULS OF BLACK FOLK, W. E. B. Du Bois. 176pp. 28041-1 $2.00
SELF-RELIANCE AND OTHER ESSAYS, Ralph Waldo Emerson. 128pp. 27790-9 $1.00
GREAT SPEECHES, Abraham Lincoln. 112pp. 26872-1 $1.00
THE PRINCE, Niccolò Machiavelli. 80pp. 27274-5 $1.00
SYMPOSIUM AND PHAEDRUS, Plato. 96pp. 27798-4 $1.00
THE TRIAL AND DEATH OF SOCRATES: FOUR DIALOGUES, Plato. 128pp. 27066-1 $1.00
CIVIL DISOBEDIENCE AND OTHER ESSAYS, Henry David Thoreau. 96pp. 27563-9 $1.00
THE THEORY OF THE LEISURE CLASS, Thorstein Veblen. 256pp. 28062-4 $2.00

PLAYS

THE CHERRY ORCHARD, Anton Chekhov. 64pp. 26682-6 $1.00
THE THREE SISTERS, Anton Chekhov. 64pp. 27544-2 $1.00
THE WAY OF THE WORLD, William Congreve. 80pp. 27787-9 $1.00
MEDEA, Euripides. 64pp. 27548-5 $1.00
THE MIKADO, William Schwenck Gilbert. 64pp. 27268-0 $1.00

DOVER · THRIFT · EDITIONS

All books complete and unabridged. All 5³⁄₁₆″ × 8¼″, paperbound.
Just $1.00–$2.00 in U.S.A.

PLAYS

FAUST, PART ONE, Johann Wolfgang von Goethe. 192pp. 28046-2 $2.00

SHE STOOPS TO CONQUER, Oliver Goldsmith. 80pp. 26867-5 $1.00

A DOLL'S HOUSE, Henrik Ibsen. 80pp. 27062-9 $1.00

HEDDA GABLER, Henrik Ibsen. 80pp. 26469-6 $1.00

VOLPONE, Ben Jonson. 112pp. 28049-7 $1.00

THE MISANTHROPE, Molière. 64pp. 27065-3 $1.00

HAMLET, William Shakespeare. 128pp. 27278-8 $1.00

JULIUS CAESAR, William Shakespeare. 80pp. 26876-4 $1.00

KING LEAR, William Shakespeare. 112pp. 28058-6 $1.00

MACBETH, William Shakespeare. 96pp. 27802-6 $1.00

A MIDSUMMER NIGHT'S DREAM, William Shakespeare. 80pp. 27067-X $1.00

ROMEO AND JULIET, William Shakespeare. 96pp. 27557-4 $1.00

ARMS AND THE MAN, George Bernard Shaw. 80pp. (Available in U.S. only.) 26476-9 $1.00

THE SCHOOL FOR SCANDAL, Richard Brinsley Sheridan. 96pp. 26687-7 $1.00

ANTIGONE, Sophocles. 64pp. 27804-2 $1.00

OEDIPUS REX, Sophocles. 64pp. 26877-2 $1.00

MISS JULIE, August Strindberg. 64pp. 27281-8 $1.00

THE PLAYBOY OF THE WESTERN WORLD AND RIDERS TO THE SEA, J. M. Synge. 80pp. 27562-0 $1.00

THE IMPORTANCE OF BEING EARNEST, Oscar Wilde. 64pp. 26478-5 $1.00

For a complete descriptive list of all volumes in the Dover Thrift Editions series
write for a free Dover Fiction and Literature Catalog (59047-X) to
Dover Publications, Inc., Dept. DTE, 31 E. 2nd Street, Mineola, NY 11501